MOTORCYCLE JOURNEYS THROUGH
NEW ENGLAND

Other Touring Guides in
The Motorcycle Journeys Series

Motorcycle Journeys Through The Alps and Corsica

Motorcycle Journeys Through The Appalachians

Motorcycle Journeys Through Baja

Motorcycle Journeys Through California

Motorcycle Vagabonding In Japan

Motorcycle Journeys Through Northern Mexico

Motorcycle Journeys Through Southern Mexico

Motorcycle Journeys Through The Southwest

Also from Whitehorse Press

Motorcycle Touring and Travel:
A Handbook of Travel by Motorcycle

MOTORCYCLE JOURNEYS THROUGH
NEW ENGLAND

Third Edition

by Marty Berke

Whitehorse Press
North Conway, New Hampshire

I dedicate this book to Pauline, Tara, and Sonia.

Front cover photo by Jeff Hackett
Interior photos by the author, Ken Aiken, and the
staff of Whitehorse Press

We recognize that some words, model names and
designations mentioned herein are the property of
the trademark holder. We use them for identification
purposes only.

Whitehorse Press books are also available at
discounts in bulk quantity for sales and promotional
use. For details about special sales or for a catalog of
motorcycling books and videos, write to the
publisher:
Whitehorse Press
107 East Conway Road
Center Conway, New Hampshire 03813-4012
Phone: 603-356-6556 or 800-531-1133
E-mail: CustomerService@WhitehorsePress.com
Internet: www.WhitehorsePress.com

ISBN 1-884313-45-0

5 4 3

Printed in the United States of America

Acknowledgments

I thank the open, honest people I meet on the road who share the feel, not just the facts, of their hometowns.

I also thank the Whitehorse Press gang, and especially Ken Aiken, author of *Touring Vermont's Scenic Roads,* for making this third edition a better and more useful book.

—*Marty Berke*

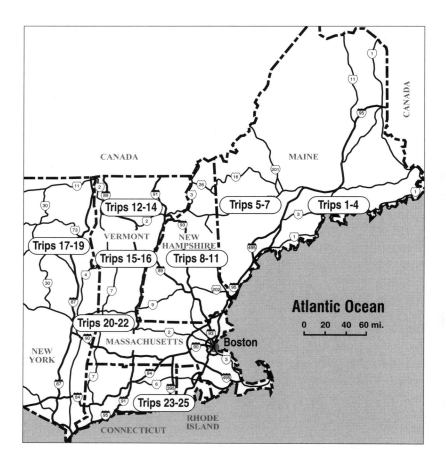

Contents

Introduction

Hey gang, who says you can never go back! I know I've changed since the first edition twelve years ago, but New England and its roads are still a motorcycling oasis on the east coast.

What's different: we've expanded the geographical coverage, updated some things that have changed, and thrown in some new curves to boot.

I do not list every bump in the road, nor even every great motorcycling road. This book, however, is written with the special needs of us motorcyclists in mind: you'll find comments on the quality of roads, service facilities, breakfast places, and other important matters. As for the routes, think of them as a starting point, giving you the benefit of my experiences while allowing you to build your own repertoire of favorite journeys. Depending on how much time you have available, the kind of terrain you prefer, and of course, your whim, you will quickly build your own custom journeys.

New England is a region of contrast and diversity. The compactness of New England allows you to venture from 6,000-foot mountain peaks to beaches on the Atlantic Ocean, and from Yankee seaports to the largest body of fresh water outside the Great Lakes—on the same day!

The variety of terrain—lakes, rivers, islands, ocean, and mountains—provides a rich backdrop for touring adventures. The mountains give us roads with tight ascending and descending curves. In the valleys you can meander through rolling farmlands that seem to go on without end, where you can't tell what's over the other side until you're there. Little-used river and lake roads hug the water's edge so tight you'd think you were riding a snake's back. Honky-tonk seaside towns sit beside the original "perpetual wave machine."

There are two general rules for choosing roads in New England. The first is that north-south routes follow rivers on valley floors. These roads will vary from sharp curves to smooth lazy turns, but they tend to be flat, while east-west roads are characterized by mountain ascents and descents, tighter curves, switchbacks, and rougher roads. The second rule: route numbers with the greater number of digits and/or with letters further down the alphabet tend to be smaller and have tighter curves. For example, Route 402 or 17F will be more fun than Route 42 or 17A!

Organization of the Book

The book contains two kinds of information: descriptions of the journeys themselves, and useful or important "on the road" information. The journeys take advantage of the compactness of New England, the variety of its terrain, and its extensive road system.

The roads in New England, like those in most older settlements of the world, tend to follow what existed before the advent of the internal combustion engine. Most of the little rural roads are paved cow paths. Although this school of road design can be a source of frustration in a city environment (as anybody will understand on a first attempt to navigate the city of Boston), in a rural setting we are grateful that cows don't walk a straight line.

Each "journey" described in this book includes three to five day-long "loops." At the beginning of each journey, an orientation section gives you a look at the geography and/or history of the particular region, something to provide a little context to the ride.

I have designed the journeys to be flexible. My objective is to expose you to New England's entire geographical menu. If you have a week or two, sip and savor the full five-loop banquet. Got a weekend? Try a couple of loops from the *a la carte* menu. Sneaking off for a day trip? Taste some of the highlights to go.

As a matter of safety, comfort, and personal preference, I like to establish a base camp so I can travel more nimbly during the day without my touring gear, and give myself more time to ride by not having to set up or break down my gear each day. I camp as much as possible because the experience immerses me in the environment. For each journey, the loops bring you back to a chosen home base. I have identified my base camps for each journey; however, there are no rules here! You can start and finish anywhere you choose. There are plenty of places to stay on these journeys. Depending on your budget and personal preferences, your choices range from campgrounds, to motels, to B&Bs, to inns. Have fun exploring!

With a few longer exceptions, each loop within a particular journey equals a day's ride. I tried to design a full day of riding for each loop, including unique places, attractions, or points of interest, and bring you back to home base.

The loops themselves average between 150 and 200 miles and will have tight twisties, open road, scenic vistas, and a place or two to stop and exercise all five senses. If your style leans toward marathon riding, try combining a couple of loops. If your style is to point to and appreciate every tree, rock, and man-made structure in the universe, you can abbreviate the loops.

I have included for each loop the directions; a loop drawing; a description of the ride; places to stay; places of interest; and finally, useful road information. Odometers vary in accuracy, so don't panic if the distance you travel differs a mite from what we have listed. The maps of the journeys are roughly to scale; however, a good road map is indispensable for finding your own special squiggly, not to mention the way home.

Dollars and Sense

I chose the loops and the places to stay, stop, or eat within the journeys based on the following criteria:

Safety. This consists of road surface, amount of four-wheel traffic, and/or remoteness. Special safety factors for a specific journey, if there are any (for example, moose in the Notches Journey), are in the orientation section for the specific journey.

Comfort. This includes physical accommodations, natural beauty and charm, and social acceptance of motorcyclists. If the place is in this book, I was well received.

Value. Assuming that most of us seek the biggest bang for our touring buck, quality of service and cost were criteria in choosing accommodations, food, and attractions. Where restaurants are mentioned, one $ is inexpensive, $$ is moderate, $$$ is expensive.

I am always interested in your opinions. If you have favorite roads to suggest, ideas to make this book better, or other helpful hints to offer, please send them along to me, care of Whitehorse Press. Thanks, and keep the rubber side down!

Finding Your Own Way

The fun begins with planning your journey. A road map contains vital information such as distances (and therefore time needed to complete a journey), road surfaces (which affect safety and comfort), and size of road (highway, byway, county, or country). The key to making the road map a useful tool is the ability to glean this information from your map and apply it to the ride. I know of nothing more frustrating than stopping every ten minutes on a bumpy dirt road, in the dark, to reaffirm membership in the "Where-The-Hell-Are-We" club.

Most maps are oriented to north as the top border. This is true for state and regional maps as well as those in this book. Double-check, however, because specific city or small geography maps may pivot the north axis for easy reading. The right margin of the map (if the top is north) is east. That's the direction the sun will be rising in the morning.

The legend, which is similar to the index of a book, allows you to convert the map pictorial into useful information. An example is the mileage scale, which converts inches to miles or kilometers. This scale allows you to plan time and distance for the trip. The boldness (thickness) of the lines correspond to the size of the road. The boldest line represents interstate highways; the thinnest lines (my favorite) represent country back roads. The more squiggly the line, the more curvy the road!

Using the map to navigate is easy if you apply a few simple techniques. First, study the map before you leave to determine the general direction to your destination. Look at the route and what is on it, for example, mountains, rivers, lakes, or grandma's house. Which landmarks make for natural resting spots? How long to the first checkpoint (both time and mileage)?

Second, orient your map to your route. Since you can read a map from any direction, place the map in your tank bag with your destination at the top. For example, if you are taking a route to the east, place the easterly border of the map on top. Now you, the map, and the terrain are all aligned. It makes for easier landmark recognition. Fold the map so that only the panel representing the route is visible. The less time you spend looking down at the map, the more time you have your eyes on the road!

Hints

1. I find that a little research at the library can add a lot of richness and depth to my experience and memories of a ride. Libraries, whether in your home town or on the road, are accessible, free, hold a wealth of useful information, and are a great place to hide out from the wet stuff!

2. The information in each journey identifies good map sources, but also stop at any local real estate office for specific county maps. These maps will show even the smallest local roads, which are often the best for exploring.

3. As you are preparing for a trip, write down your route before you leave and place it in a corner of your map holder with one of those less-than-permanent sticky note pads, large enough to read yet small enough not to interfere with your map. List the route numbers in order. For example, the Northeast Notches loop directions would be 16n-26e-2w-113s-302w-16s. This will give you intersection references without making you orient yourself to the map at each interchange.

4. An excellent guide to the sport of motorcycle touring, with help on selecting equipment, packing, dressing properly, handling emergencies, and general road smarts, is the book *Motorcycle Touring and Travel,* by Bill Stermer, available from Whitehorse Press, P.O. Box 60, North Conway, NH 03860-0060, www.WhitehorsePress.com

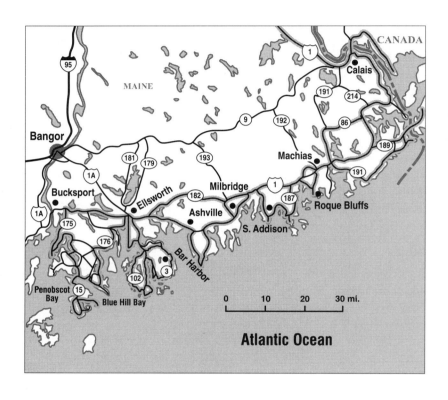

Goin' Downeast

Maine, the largest of the six New England states, has a total area about the size of the other five states combined. One county, Aroostook, is larger than Connecticut and Rhode Island together. This journey will easily take five days, not including travel to and from Mt. Desert Island, our home base.

The state is 320 miles long, but exploring the harbors, coves, points, and peninsulas of the shoreline (3,478 miles) is the equivalent of driving cross-country. Because of the forces of moon, sun, tides, weather, and their interaction with this vast shoreline, a number of natural attractions are a question of timing. For example, East Quoddy Head Light on Campobello Island can only be reached during the 1-1/2 hours on either side of slack tide. You can pick up tidal charts at most local tourist centers. I highlight the cosmic timing, along with the attraction it affects, in the loop descriptions. Slack tide is dead low tide and flood tide is high tide.

Maine is the largest blueberry-growing state in the nation (don't worry, blueberry pancakes are discussed in the individual loops). It is nationally famed for its lobsters; 90 percent of the nation's lobsters are caught along the Maine coast, amounting to more than 50 million pounds a year. Fishing is a huge industry in Maine. The catch each year includes more than 100 million pounds of fin fish and 10 million pounds of shellfish. Get ready for some good downeast riding and down-home eating!

Take that perfect lighthouse photo at East Quoddy Head Light.

Before you take off, you should have these tidbits of information. First, Maine drivers have a peculiar habit of using at least two-thirds of the available road surface to get from one place to another. You often see signs warning KEEP TO RIGHT. Please do so, because Maine drivers don't! Anticipate and take the inside line on all curves.

Second: Downeast Maine has its own language. The following dictionary of terms will help you understand directions, make conversation, and prevent you from saying "huh?" a million times. Thanks to "Bob the Lobster" at **Ruth & Wimpy's Kitchen** for his patience in teaching a fromaway (a foreigner, not from the state of Maine).

ablow—wind; that is, "Look out, its going to be a whopper of ablow"

apiece—a further; a measurement; for example, "Down the rud apiece"

ayah—yes, most of the time; it does not necessarily mean agreement

boondocks—land more than 500 yards from the shore

butt-sprung—condition of aged male whose rear end drags

by thunder—an expletive; cuss word

cah—something to contain lobsters being held for market; an auto

camp—Maine person's cottage

cottage—summer person's mansion

crik—small stream; pain in the neck

cripes—candy-coated cuss word

crittah—any animal, including Democrats

cussed—term of endearment used to describe "fromaways"

flats—land offshore, fragrant at low tide

gaud—cuss word, mostly directed at elected officials

in full sail—a well-endowed female

lowry—overcast weather; sourpuss

messo—unit o' measurement; for example, "Messo clams"

mite—much or many

pound—place where lobsters are stored; a unit o' measurement

reach—long body o' water between hunks of land

rud—highway, byway

shuck—to divest clams of their innards to make chowdah!

spleeny—milk-toast type; coward; applied mostly to husbands

summah—between spring and fall

tunk—to hit; for example, "Tunk it a mite"

yad—land in front of or around house

The third piece of important information is how and where to eat lobster. The only type of establishment that counts when you eat Maine lobster is a lobster pound. You will recognize a lobster pound by the billowing smokestacks and steam rising from large washbasins of boiling sea water. As you enter the wooden shack, you are immediately enveloped by the aroma of chowdah, buttah, steamahs (clams), and, of course, lobstahs. The sharp cracks coming from the long wooden family-style tables tweak your interest about what's going on o' yondah. As you approach the "order here" counter, you watch the small net bags of red lobsters returning from their fate, being grabbed by . . . *number four!* The menu is a la carte, written on the blackboard. You buy your soft drinks, corn, butter, and bread individually.

When it's your turn, address the cooler or salt-water trough with your index finger poised, and begin the hunt for your main course. Focus, aim, aannd . . . point. You order and buy the lobster by the pound (make sure it's hard shell because they molt). Two pounds is a good meal, three is gluttonous, four is a massacre (and a tougher tasting bird).

The wait person will net and bag your choice, give you a number, carry your catch to the salt-water vats you passed on the way in, and drop them in. You'll get a call in about 12 to 15 minutes. You will receive your lobster in a baking pan similar to a corn bread pan. This is your dinner plate. Tear off the claws, grab your nutcracker, and join the cacophony of the dining room. There is meat in the claws, in the knuckles attached to the claws, in the small eight legs, inside the body at the junction of the small legs and body (don't eat the gray fibrous pieces, they're the lungs), and in the tail. Don't forget the five little fantails. It is a messy, sensual experience, and everybody gets into it. There is usually a communal sink in the dining room to hose yourself down. *Bon appetit!*

Our home base for the Downeast Journey is the **Mt. Desert Campground** on Mt. Desert Island. Note: although the name of this popular area is spelled like an arid place, it is pronounced like the diet-buster. Nestled at the top of Somes Sound, most sites have platforms, many sitting high above or directly on the water. The scent of the ocean and the cry of a gull reflect the journey's theme.

The first chance you get upon arrival on Mt. Desert Island, pick up a copy of the *Acadia Weekly*. This free weekly publication is a combination almanac and tourist guide. It lists sunrise, sunset, high, and low tides for each day of that week. All of these will come in handy as timing, as we all know, can be of the utmost importance when visiting various island attractions. It includes a dining and entertainment guide, suggested activities, maps, houses of worship, and, of course, advertisements from many of the fine local tourist traps. Also included are listings for the Acadia Park Ranger programs, which are a great way to see and learn more about the local ecology, geology, and history.

Trip 1   Sunrise County Loop

Distance *251 to 420 miles*

Highlights *Riding along sweeping ocean views, small back roads through pine forests, and through small villages and harbors make for a memorable time.*

The Route from Mt. Desert Campground

0 mi. From Mt. Desert Campground turn left onto Route 198 north

0.9 At Somesville, turn right onto Route 102/198 north

5.3 At traffic light, turn left onto Route 3 west

13.7 In Ellsworth (at Rite Aid), turn right onto Route 1 north

30.8 A couple miles beyond Ashville, turn right onto Route 186 south

You'll have plenty of opportunities to stop and take pictures of the breathtaking Maine coastline. Places like East Quoddy Head Light provide great picnic stops.

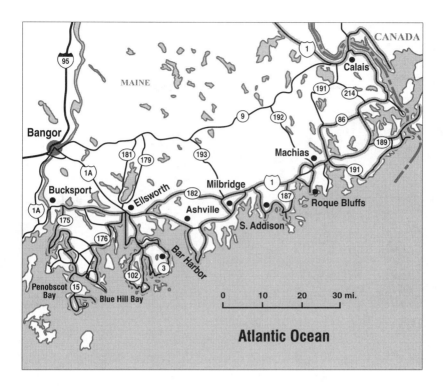

37.3 At Winter Harbor, turn left to stay on Route 186

37.9 (For a side trip to look at Acadia National Park, turn right at this point; the loop through the park is about 6.5 miles, ending at Birch Harbor; otherwise continue east on Route 186.) (See text for side trip to Acadia National Park.)

39.6 At Birch Harbor, the loop through Acadia Park rejoins Route 186

46.8 At Gouldsboro, turn right to rejoin Route 1 north

57.1 In Milbridge, turn right onto Route 1A north

64.7 At Harrington, keep straight ahead to rejoin Route 1 north

67.3 Turn right onto Saco Road toward Addison

69.0 Keep right and follow signs to South Addison on access road (no name)

69.4 Turn left in front of the Volunteer Fire Station

75.8 Near South Addison, turn left onto Basin Road; you will be heading northeast to the village of Indian River

81.8 Turn right onto Route 187 south at Indian River

These lobster traps are empty because I'm full.

85.6 At T in West Jonesport take a left (no sign for 187 continuation). (See text for side trip to Beals Island.)

98.2 Turn right onto Route 1 north at junction

99.8 At Jonesboro, bear right onto old US Route 1 north, following ROQUE BLUFFS STATE PARK sign

100.6 At Y go right; follow signs to Roque Bluffs State Park

105.3 Turn right and follow signs to state park

107.8 At the water in Roque Bluffs State Park; return by same access road

113.0 In Kennebec, turn left toward Machias

115.3 Bear right at fork onto Route 1 north (follow sign for MACHIAS)

120.9 At East Machias, bear right onto Route 191 east

145.3 At South Trescott, turn right (follow coast) where Route 191 bears left

150.9 At the causeway near Quoddy Head State Park, follow signs to Route 189 east and Lubec. (See text for side trip to Quoddy Head State Park.)

153.7 At Lubec, turn left onto Route 189 west (See text for side trip through Lubec and over the Canadian border to Campobello Island.)

163.7 At Whiting, turn left onto Route 1 south (See text for side trip to Eastport and Calais.)

176.4 If you took the side trip to Eastport and Calais, you will rejoin Route 1 south here at East Machias, coming from Route 191. Continue south on Route 1

180.4 At Machias, turn right onto Route 1A south

188.2 At junction with Route 1, turn right onto Route 1 south

209.4 At Cherryfield, turn right onto Route 182 west

232.8 At junction with Route 1, turn right onto Route 1 south

237.5 At Ellsworth, turn left onto Route 3 east

245.9 At junction with Route 198, turn right onto Route 98/102 south

250.2 At Somesville, turn left onto Route 198 south

251.2 Return to campground

Side Trip to Acadia National Park

0 mi. From Route 186, turn right onto Moore Road toward the park; follow Moore Road and Schoodic Road through the park

6.5 At Birch Harbor, rejoin Route 186; turn right to continue east on main route

The road to Schoodic Point leads you past dramatic views of the ocean to the easternmost portion of Acadia National Park.

Side Trip to Beals Island

0 mi. From Route 187 in Jonesport, turn right toward Beals Island at Beals Island Bridge, then left onto coastal road

5.2 At end of road, turn around and return by same route

10.4 Turn right to rejoin Route 187 north

Side Trip to Quoddy Head State Park

0 mi. From the junction of Boot Cove Road and South Lubec Road, take a right over the causeway (almost a 180-degree turn) to Quoddy Head Road and Quoddy Head State Park

1.9 At Quoddy Head State Park, turn around and leave by the same route

3.8 Bear right at intersection of Quoddy Head Road. Follow signs to Route 189 east and Lubec

Side Trip through Lubec to Campobello Island in Canada

0 mi. From the junction of South Lubec Road and Route 189, turn right onto Route 189 east toward the Canadian border at Campobello Island, New Brunswick

The FDR Memorial Bridge in Lubec is the gateway to Campobello Island in Canada.

1.3 Cross Canadian border and onto Route 774 east; bear right at T. Follow signs for WILSON'S BEACH and HEAD HARBOR to East Quoddy Head.

8.3 At end of road, return via Route 774 west

15.3 Cross U.S. border via Route 774 west to Route 189 west

16.6 Return to junction of South Lubec Road. Continue west on Route 189 to resume main route

Side Trip to Eastport and Calais

0 mi. From Whiting, turn right onto Route 1 north

20.4 At Perry, turn right onto Route 190 east

27.8 Turn around at Eastport

35.5 Left on Route 1 south at Perry (See Detour 2)

56.2 At Calais, cross Canadian border, then rejoin Route 1 north at Saint Stephen, New Brunswick

65.5 Turn right onto Route 127 south at junction

75.5 Arrive at Saint Andrews (by-the-sea); return by same route

85.2 Turn left onto Route 1 south

94.7 At Calais, cross back into the United States and continue south on Route 1

115.3 At Perry, Maine, continue south on Route 1

126.4 Near Dennysville, bear right onto Route 86 west and south

136.8 At junction with Route 191, turn left onto Route 191 east

146.9 At East Machias, turn right onto Route 1 south and rejoin main route

The Sunrise County Loop has so many things to see along the way that you should consider doing it as a two- or three-day trip. Even that amount of time doesn't give you enough opportunity to absorb the grandeur and subtle beauty of the easternmost section of the United States, with its projection into the North Atlantic. If you can afford to linger, I offer plenty of options and side trips to fill the time.

On my first night at the campground, I fell asleep to the sound of a comforting and enveloping foghorn, not realizing what it portended for the morning: fog. Fog is common in Maine, but you can keep it from restricting your travel by starting your trip inland. This loop can be ridden in reverse order so you reach the best scenery later in the day, after the fog has burnt off.

As you leave Mt. Desert Island via Route 3 over the Thompson Island Bridge and flats, you will run through a gauntlet of establishments catering

There's something yummy for the tummy at Trenton Bridge Lobster Pound.

to the summer vacation trade. There's every version of good family fun imaginable: ice cream, mini-golf, water slides, laser tag, you name it. Among this tourist litter is a string of lobster pounds. The best for value with the largest selection is **Trenton Bridge Lobster Pound,** just over the bridge on the mainland. Lunch or dinner, the blackboard menu reads lobster. A cloud of saltwater steam hovers around the place from the large wood-fired cookers out front.

Route 1 north provides glimpses of Frenchman Bay and, on a clear day, the silhouette of the mountains on Mt. Desert Island. Route 186 leads you down Schoodic Peninsula to Winter Harbor and the easternmost portion of Acadia National Park. Take a right onto the 6.5-mile, one-way park road around Schoodic Point. The primeval spruce forest abuts the shoreline, where unstoppable ocean waves crash endlessly against the immovable granite coast. Just after a storm and/or in conjunction with a full moon, the tide is particularly dramatic (bring your rain gear, as the ocean spray makes you feel like you have the forward watch on the prow). It's worth a full roll of film. Acadia National Park shares the peninsula with a large naval communications facility.

Rejoin Route 186 and grab Route 1 north to continue your game of hide-and-seek with the coast. In Milbridge, bear right onto Route 1A, a less-traveled road that cuts through the salt marshes of Narraguagus and Pleasant Bays to Harrington. **Perry's Seafood** on Route 1 is a good place to fill up on the house special: a seafood omelet almost as big as your head.

About three-quarters of a mile up Route 1 from Perry's, you will come to a crossroad intersection. Take a right onto Saco Road toward Addison and South Addison. About two miles later, bear left at the Addison Volunteer Fire Dept. This little mini-loop brings you in and around lovely salt marshes and quaint little coves with nothing but lobster pot floats to indicate civilization is close at hand. About six and a half miles beyond the fire station, turn left onto Basin Rd., toward Route 187 north and Jonesport, a picturesque harbor best appreciated from Beals Island.

(See Side Trip to Beal's Island.)

➡ Side Trip to Beals Island

Take a left over the bridge and head on over to Beals Island with plenty of film in your camera (or space on your memory card). These are real working towns and the graying weathered wharves piled high with lobster traps and markers and other half-sorted piles of paraphernalia look exactly like you'd imagine they would. ■

Back on Route 1 north, just after the town of Jonesboro, bear right toward Roque Bluffs State Park. The park is six miles off Route 1. It has one of the few sandy beaches on the rocky Maine coast. Just across the street from the saltwater beach, you can rinse in a fresh-water pond. That is, if you dare go for a brisk 55-degree-average-ocean-temperature dip! It's a place to stretch your legs and get rid of "NumButt," although with the water that cold, you'll probably be numb again in no time. The Park has a modest admission fee.

Returning to Route 1 north, passing through the town of Machias, pick up any provisions you need. It is the last sizable town on the loop with reasonable prices for commodities such as batteries and film.

Route 191 south, starting east of Machias, is an exceptional road. Smooth and isolated, it hugs the craggy shoreline at a height that provides ocean vistas the entire way to West Quoddy Head. Those high towers off to the south just after North Cutler, which look like the superstructure to a football stadium, are an array of radio towers. This 2,800-acre U.S. Navy base provides communications to all units of the fleet in the North Atlantic, Arctic, and Europe. There are 26 major towers forming two arrays. Each center tower is 980 feet tall, just 40 feet shorter than the Empire State Building.

Almost 25 miles after picking up Route 191, turn right in South Trescott onto unmarked Boot Cove Road, just as Route 191 veers inland toward West Lubec. After the split, you come to Bailey's Mistake, a small coastal harbor. Captain Bailey, it seems, made the mistake (with considerable use of his sextant and compass one foggy night) of running aground seven miles off course from the Lubec Narrows. The next morning, under clear skies, Captain Bailey could see he was in the center of a mile-wide bay and not in the Narrows between Lubec and Campobello Island. With his ego in worse shape than his ship, the captain and crew unloaded their timber cargo, built homes, and never returned to their home port of Boston.

➡ Side Trip to West Quoddy Head Lighthouse

Follow the road out to West Quoddy Head Lighthouse, the easternmost point in the continental United States. This park is a must-see. The candy-striped lighthouse was built in 1858. The beacon, 83 feet above sea level, can be seen for twenty miles. The lighthouse and pathways sit on top of 90-foot cliffs, and binoculars come in handy for spotting the humpback and northern right whales that migrate from the northeastern coast of South America to this part of the Bay of Fundy each summer to mate and calve. The waves crash on outcrops both near and far, and seals play or sun themselves on these small oases. A constant reminder of danger, the groaner buoy, one mile offshore, sounds a continuous warning for Sail Rock. Depending on the weather, you can spot the Canadian Islands of Campobello and Grand Manan. There is a modest fee to use the walking trails.

Not quite two miles after leaving West Quoddy Head, turn right to cut northward toward Lubec. ■

(See Side Trip to West Quoddy Head Lighthouse.)

Lubec is the easternmost *town* in the United States, although Eastport, on the other side of Cobscook Bay, lays claim to the title of the easternmost *city* in the United States. Actually, the Aleutian Islands are the easternmost part of the U.S., since a part of them are across the international date line in the Pacific. You probably should not mention that small detail in either Eastport or Lubec.

Lubec's main claim to fame, though, is being the gateway to Campobello Island, the childhood summer home of Franklin Delano Roosevelt. It was here that he contracted polio and was carried off the island; he made only two visits afterward.

(See Side Trip to Campobello Island)

Upon returning to the U.S., grab Route 189 out of Lubec and head west toward Whiting, where it merges with Route 1 south (follow signs). As with all these roads, you'll note that there is very little shoulder. Maine drivers, whether they be of the true Yankee order ("no need to throw out that old truck, you can fix it") or a member of the summer population in shiny SUVs, tend to hedge their bets a bit by riding close to (over) the centerline on these rural roads. Take extra caution around blind corners and over rises and give yourself plenty of time to react to the unexpected.

(See Side Trip to Eastport)

On Routes 191, 1, and 1A south of Machias, on the north side of the road, you'll notice a curious, low-brush, almost surreal moonscape. These are the famed blueberry barrens of Maine. In late summer, these rolling flatlands are a sea of blue. During late August, local and migrant workers (mostly the Micmac Indian tribe from New Brunswick) work from dawn to dusk to harvest the entire blueberry crop in three to four weeks. In mid- to late Septem-

The Roosevelt summer cottage and its tour allow a glimpse of how FDR lived away from Washington D.C.

➡ Side Trip to Campobello Island

To visit Campobello Island, cross over the FDR Memorial Bridge. You are leaving the United States and you must stop for Canadian Immigration and Customs. Ditto on the return with the U.S. entry. The Canadian requirements for entry by U.S. citizens is a passport or birth certificate with photo ID. The U.S. requirement for entry by Canadian citizens for visitor status is the same. If you are neither a U.S. nor a Canadian citizen, please call U.S. and Canadian Immigration departments for your requirements.

Stop at the information booth on the right just up the road apiece. The attendants have maps, tidal charts, and information on the island attractions, New Brunswick, and Canada. The two major attractions on Campobello Island are the Roosevelt Campobello International Park and the East Quoddy Head Light.

The free park has a 15-minute orientation film on the history of FDR and his relationship with Campobello Island. The "summer cottage" is refurbished in actual period pieces. The tour guides embellish the history with flair and enthusiasm. It is easy to imagine yourself playing and living in the cottage as a kid.

East Quoddy Head Light is seven miles past the Park at the end of the island (bear right at T). If you time it to arrive at slack tide (about 1-1/2 hours on either side of low tide), you can climb a series of metal ladders to get to the lighthouse. The views are sterling, with harbors on both sides of the point, lobster boats pulling up their traps, and fishing boats returning from the sea with gulls whirling above in the wind. An excursion worth the dismount. A note of cosmic caution: the tide rises five feet an hour. If you get caught on the point, you'll have to wait eight or nine hours before you can return. ■

ber the barrens ignite into flame red and scarlet, turning their majestic fall colors earlier than the rest of the surrounding foliage.

In Harrington, bear right onto Route 1 south and follow it to Cherryfield, where you will bear right onto Route 182 west, a Maine scenic highway that fords streams, cuts across Tunk Lake, and offers the same untamed beauty inland as Maine offers on its shores.

It is a straightforward jaunt home from here.

➡ Side Trip to Eastport

There are so many things to do and see along this route that I encourage you to take as much time as you need to enjoy everything. If your schedule allows you extra days, I recommend you leave Lubec and drive the 40 miles around Cobscook Bay to Eastport, a picturesque sea town. Route 190 is a long causeway with lovely views of spruce-dotted islands. Water Street in Eastport, the main drag, runs parallel to the ocean, 20 feet from tides that range from 16 to 22 feet. One of the effects of these extreme tides is Old Sow, the second largest whirlpool in the world and one of the most dangerous. Created by tidal currents coming together between Eastport and Deer Island, New Brunswick, Old Sow has tipped over a tanker and swallowed many small ships. To see it, take a left on Water Street (as you face the ocean) out to the Bayview Cemetery, or off Clark Street. Old Sow is best seen about an hour and a half before flood tide between Dog Island Point and Deer Island, N.B. Another good spot for observing tidal flows is Reversing Falls in West Pembroke.

Returning, head west on Route 190, then take Route 1 south and pick up Route 86 west, a small swath of asphalt cut through some very large pine stands. The curves come quickly and then the road straightens, then tight curves return, then it's back to wailing. Route 86 and Route 191 that follow are a typical example of the "Maine bomber negotiating corners without heed to oncoming traffic" syndrome. Caveat Rider! ■

Near Machias, you'll notice these strange fields of low brushes. They are the blueberry barrens.

Trip 2   Bar Harbor-Acadia National Park Loop

Distance   *45 miles*

Highlights   *Scenic ocean views, lakes, ponds, cliffs and mountains from sea level to highest point on the entire North American Atlantic coast*

The Route from Mt. Desert Campground

0 mi   From Mt. Desert Campground turn left onto Route 198 north

0.9   At Somesville, turn right onto Route 102/198 north

3.8   At Town Hill, turn right onto Crooked Road

9.0   Turn right onto Route 3 south

9.4   Turn right onto Paradise Hill Road

12.4   Turn left onto Park Loop Road (Jordan Pond Road)

30.2   Turn right onto Cadillac Summit Road

The views from Precipice trail on Mt. Desert Island are awe-inspiring. Here you can see a cruise ship docked in the harbor.

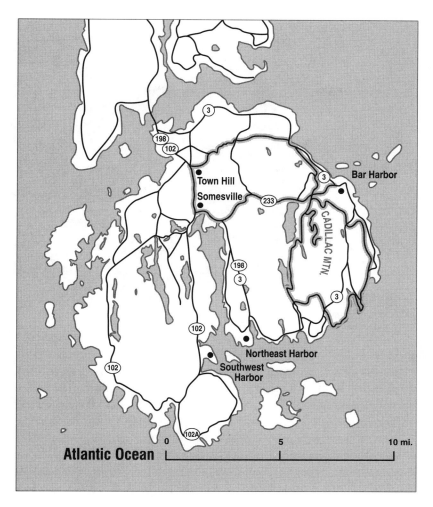

33.7 Turn around at summit and head back down

37.1 Turn right onto Park Loop Road (Jordan Pond Road)

37.7 Turn left onto Paradise Hill Road

38.0 Turn right to exit onto Route 233, then left onto Route 233 east

39.1 In Bar Harbor, turn around and return on Route 233 west

45.0 Turn right onto Route 198 (SR 3)

45.4 Turn left into campground

Acadia National Park is the second most visited national park in the United States. Over four million people play in the park yearly. Do not be fooled by

Just off Main Street and a stone's throw from Northeast Harbor's marina you'll find the Docksider, a quaint spot to grab some great coastal New England eats.

the mileage or speed of the Park Loop. The park beckons you to stop and explore with all your senses. It is a full day and night of geological splendor. A few suggestions: if you are going in July or August, do the loop before 10 a.m. or after 4 p.m., over a couple of days. The entry fee is $5.00 for a week!

The Loop Road is a two-lane, well-paved road. About two-thirds of the loop is one-way. Parking is allowed in the right-hand lane. Watch for people opening their driver's door without looking! You can and will want to stop every half-mile. I found the safest way to negotiate the traffic and pedestrians is to stay in the left-hand lane, put on my left blinker, and let everybody deal with passing right, around me. This is a challenging loop to practice your slow race skills. Take your time.

I found that wearing sneakers, although sacrificing a little protection, made the day's roam on foot easier than wearing my riding boots. Bring a picnic lunch; the choices of where to dine in the outdoors are unparalleled and unlimited.

The loop begins at the visitor's center, where you can get a preview of the day's ride. The visitor's center has an excellent topographical model for orientation and sells a motorist's guide to the loop that provides a synopsis of the 13 most popular scenic spots and walking trails. The trails range from a pleasant 0.3 mile shore path along the 90-foot Otter Cliffs (I've seen pilot whales from the cliffs) to the iron rungs and ladders of the Precipice Trail.

Be sure to read about the next stop before moving on; the guide contains information designed to alert you to features along the route, not just each stop on the route.

My two favorite spots are the **Jordan Pond House** and the **Cadillac Mountain Summit Road.** The Jordan Pond House is a civilized oasis in a wild and natural setting. The restaurant, which is two-thirds around the loop, serves tea and popovers on the back lawn every day from 2:30 to 5:00 p.m. The backdrop is the cliffs of Penobscot Mountain to the west, Bubble Mountain directly ahead to the north (a couple of miles up the road from Jordan Pond you can see Balanced Rock teetering on the ledge), and Pemetic

Near Bass Harbor Head Light are many typical coastal scenes and places to stop and enjoy your surroundings.

Motorcyclists love the Park Loop Road because it provides opportunities to stop and chat with other motorcylists, while enjoying the scenery.

Mountain on the east. In the valley between is Jordan Pond, which laps the lawn by your table.

Cadillac Mountain is named for Antonine de la Mothe Cadillac, the Frenchman who took possession of this island in the late 1600s under a grant from Louis XIV. Later he founded Detroit, inspiring the name of the prestigious automobile. Cadillac Mountain, its summit, and the road to get you there will become very familiar to you, as you will climb the mountain many times. The climb, besides being a fun road with many switchbacks and cliff hangers, is one of the best ways to greet the sunrise and sunset. From Cadillac Mountain—at 1,530 feet, the highest point on the Atlantic Ocean north of Rio de Janeiro—you can be one of the first people in the United States to see a spectacular sunrise. And the next time you climb the mountain, you can see a magnificent sunset over the western part of the island. The barren granite summit, open until midnight with very little traffic after sunset, offers a surreal moonscape with vistas of Bar Harbor and the Atlantic.

If your astronomical timing is right, exactly two miles up the mountain, from the entrance to Summit Road, on the left, is a lookout where I saw an orange-crimson sunset to the west and a full moon rising in the east. I didn't know whether to howl or meditate! When I returned to the summit around 11:00 p.m., the wind was rising to 35 or 40 mph. The two other people on the summit were chilled by the wind and sea air and left as soon as they arrived.

As I was dressed for a 60-mph wind chill factor anyway, I stayed to enjoy seeing my moon shadow dancing to the cosmic rhythms.

Hint: when the summit is crowded, go just behind the tourist shop to a trail head. Cross over the trail to the outcrop of rocks and you will discover two things: the crowds are about 300 yards away in the tourist-designated summit area, and you are about five feet higher. Just in front of the radio towers, on the outcrop where you are standing, is a rock formation that looks placed. It is the U.S. Geological Marker for the summit!

Use Bar Harbor as a way station to and from your Cadillac Mountain jaunts. Bar Harbor is the commercial hub of the island, with many places to eat. In the evening, many establishments have live entertainment.

Geddy's on Main Street, down by the harbor, has an outdoor backyard game room and features live entertainment every night. A gift shop offering "Geddy Gear" fills the basement.

The Casino, on Main Street by the park, offers live music on weekends and a singer/guitarist on weekday nights.

The Lompoc Cafe, off Cottage Street, offers folk/mountain music. In the building next door, the cafe makes Bar Harbor Real Ale in its microbrewery. Tours are offered. The beer is very good, so plan to stay in one of the many inns or motels within walking distance if you decide to try it! The food is excellent, with a spicy hummus worth trying. The espresso and dessert bar make this a favorite late-night spot.

The Unusual Cabaret is just that. They offer fresh pastas each day with a serving of talented waiters and waitresses putting on musical plays after dinner.

And, if you really want to be *bad,* the **Chocolate Emporium,** on Main Street opposite Cottage Street, is unbelievable. The aroma, display, and the actual creation of the delights on the premises prohibit you from leaving without gorging yourself on the light chocolate, dark chocolate, and everything in between. Consider yourself forewarned!

Trip 3 Mt. Desert Island Loop

Distance *61 miles*

Highlights *Open ocean, seawall and coastal riding, harbors, mountains and lake vistas*

The Route from Mt. Desert Campground

0 mi From Mt. Desert Campground, turn left onto Route 198 north

0.9 At Somesville, turn right onto 102/198 north

3.1 Turn left onto Indian Point Road (first left after Town Hill Store)

4.9 Bear right at fork

8.9 At stop sign, go left

9.2 Bear right at fork onto Pretty Marsh Road/102 south (also called Seal Cove Road)

17.9 Stay straight to join 102A south

18.2 At stop sign go left to continue on 102A south

24.8 At stop sign go right onto 102 north

31.8 Turn right onto 198 south

32.5 (Pass Mt. Desert Campground on right)

Sargent's Drive by Somes Sound is another ride of conflict between watching the road and watching the scenery. Compromise by pulling over frequently.

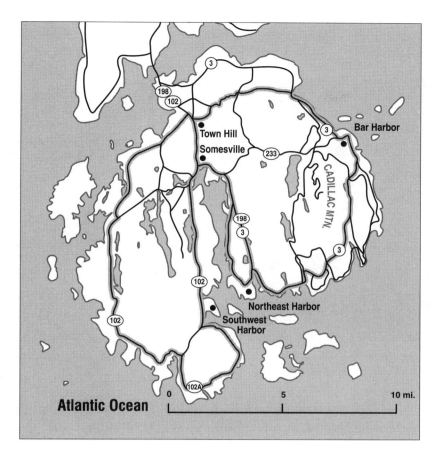

34.4 Turn right onto Sargent Drive

38.4 Turn left at stop sign at end of Sargent Drive onto Summit Road

38.5 Turn left onto Harbourside Road/Main Street/Route 198

39.5 Turn right onto Route 3 south

42.5 Turn left to continue on Route 3

50.7 Turn left onto Route 3 (in center of town)

51.2 Turn right onto Route 3 west

54.0 Turn left onto Crooked Road

58.8 Turn left onto 198/102 south

60.9 Turn left onto 3W/198 south

61.7 Turn left into Mt. Desert Campground

Looking out over the water from Moorings Restaurant in Southwest Harbor, you might wonder where the buoys and gulls are.

The western side of Mt. Desert Island has more quiet harbors and year-round residents and fewer commercial developments and tourists. It is just this lack of attention that appeals after battling the old tourist shuffle. The road to Pretty Marsh, a local favorite, runs through the pine forest on the way to the lowlands in the west. Pretty Marsh Harbor is a very small boat launch and not much else.

Just after rejoining Route 102, you'll come to the Pretty Marsh picnic area, a serene, wooded spot on the ocean. In fact, all of Route 102 down to Bass Harbor is empty of anything retail. All the roads on the east side of Route 102 are either dirt or turn to dirt soon after you get on them. Route 102 itself has sweeping curves with a couple of hard turns and no interruptions all the way to Bass Harbor.

The Bass Harbor Head Light, the southernmost point on Mt. Desert Island, is anticlimactic compared to others but is easy to get in and out to see.

Staying on Route 102A brings us to my favorite spot on this loop. The Ship Harbor Nature Trail is a 1.6-mile nature trail that opens up on the sea. The point faces south for sunning and the pink granite rocks are flat. The rocks where you sit seem to be contoured to your body. It's a good spot to nap, especially after breakfast and a stroll, with the sun warming your bones. The loop is short enough that you can take time for these types of digressions. The tough part is getting up to explore all the tidal pools. Rocks that are underwater in any part of the tidal flow are very slippery!

Route 102A continues past the Seawall Campground, one of two federal campgrounds in Acadia National Park. The campground gets its name from the natural seawall built up over time just up the road. The picnic area across from the campground is a good place to see this formation.

Just before the village of Southwest Harbor, on the southern shore, is Manset, a one-working-street complex of restaurants, the Hinkley shipyard, and marina. The Moorings Restaurant boasts a "billion-dollar view." The pier offers the same view for less money. Watch the ships in dry dock being pulled in and out of the water.

Southwest Harbor is home to shipbuilders and a Coast Guard station. Opposite the Coast Guard station is Beals Lobster Wharf, where you can eat a lobster roll right on the pier. Just off Main Street is the Wendell Gilley Museum of Bird Carving. The museum houses an impressive display of Gilley's creations along with those of other noted carvers.

Try the waters of Echo Lake in Acadia National Park.

Route 102 out of Southwest Harbor passes Echo Lake (good for swimming) and heads straight into Somesville, the oldest village on the island. Built at the headwaters of Somes Sound (the only fjord in the continental United States), the village has a historical society and is home to the Acadia Repertory Theater. Rounding Somes Sound and heading south you pick up Sargent Drive, which parallels the Sound. Trailers and campers are excluded from the road and turnouts make stopping easy.

As you head south on Sargent Drive, getting closer to Northeast Harbor, you can see mailboxes but no houses to go with them. Northeast Harbor is the wealthiest place on Mt. Desert Island. The harbor is the usual turnaround spot for people sailing up the Maine coast.

The Colonel's Restaurant on Main Street offers excellent food at reasonable prices. You have to walk down the alley between two buildings to get to the restaurant. I had the broiled haddock filet, a large piece of *fresh* fish on a homemade roll. The storefront is the Colonels' bakery, with outstanding

Watch for the "other" Colonels Restaurant at Northeast Harbor. This one has fresh fish on rolls which are made in their own bakery.

Asticou Azalea gardens in Northeast Harbor can be a peaceful, relaxing way to take a break from your ride.

desserts. The hermit (a raisin gingerbread cookie) was huge, with a strong, almost hot flavor.

Asticou Azalea Gardens, located just north of the intersection of Route 3 and 198 at the head of Northeast Harbor, is a great place to stop, stretch your legs, and enjoy one of the finest botanical collections on the island. Here you can wander along the sand paths through sunny clearings and shaded woods, along flowing streams and lily ponds, or just sit and rest upon the stone benches while taking in the sights and smells. Make sure to check out the ever-changing Japanese sand garden. This is a solemn place where you can easily get away from the rest of the world and its worries, at least for a short while. They do ask for a small $2 donation on the honor system at the entrance.

Route 3 east takes you back to Bar Harbor through Acadia. The road has lots of sweeping turns and twists. It is the best sustained bike riding road on the island. Besides, how can you resist another ride to Cadillac Mountain and a road named Crooked?

Trip 4   Blue Hill and East Penobscot Bay Loop

Distance   *155 miles without side trips*

Highlights   *Beautiful countryside, dramatic coastline, islands, and villages that range from bustling to bucolic*

The Route from Mt. Desert Campground

0 mi   From Mt. Desert Campground, turn left onto Route 198 north

0.9 mi   At Somesville, turn right onto Route 102/198 north

5.3   At traffic light, turn left onto Route 3 west

6.4   After Trenton Bridge Lobster Pound, turn left onto Route 230 north

20.5   At Ellsworth, turn left onto Route 1 south and get in left turning lane

20.8   Turn left onto Route 172 south

27.3   At Surry, turn left onto Route 176 south

37.5   At Blue Hill, turn left onto Route 175/172 south

38.4   Where Routes 172 and 175 split, turn left onto Route 175 south and west

Bass Harbor, or Bass Hahbah as the locals say it, is a good place to watch the fisherman bring in their catch.

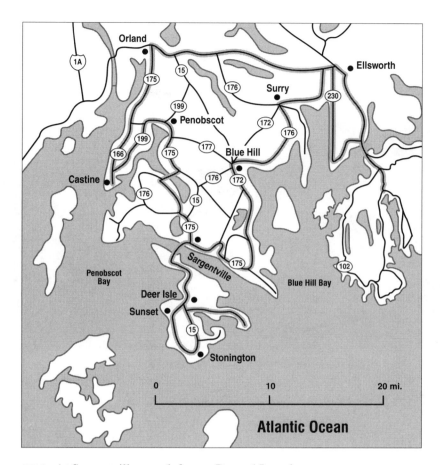

59.0   At Sargentville, turn left onto Route 15 south

72.9   After driving through Stonington, turn right onto Sand Beach Road

74.4   Bear left onto Sunset Avenue

77.8   At Sunset, bear right onto Route 15A (see text for variation)

79.7   At Deer Isle, turn left onto Route 15 north

90.0   Turn left onto Route 175 north and west

102.7   At Penobscot, turn left onto Route 199 south

106.2   Turn left onto Route 166 south

108.9   Near Castine, turn right onto Route 166A

112.7   At junction, turn left onto Route 166

114.6   At West Penobscot, turn left onto Route 175 north

Bucolic Morgan Bay is just one of many coastal scenes on this journey.

122.7   Near Orland, turn right onto Route 1 north

141.4   At Ellsworth, turn right onto Route 3 south

149.8   Turn right onto 102 south

154.1   Turn left onto 198

154.9   Turn left into campground

The Blue Hill Peninsula, Deer Isle, and East Penobscot Bay areas are the antithesis of the Mt. Desert Island, Bar Harbor bustle. The distances are longer, rural, and pristine. The largest town, off Route 1 on the loop, is Castine (and that's four streets by five streets).

Island hop across Eggemoggin Reach to Little Deer Isle, Deer Isle, Sunshine, and Mountainville over narrow causeways where the wind can whip up surf and sea spray as you fight cross currents. Other roads are smooth as silk gliding up, over, and down Union River, Blue Hill, and Penobscot Bays.

You leave Mt. Desert Island by the now familiar Routes 198, 102, and 3. Then grab Route 230, up the road apiece from the Thompson Island Bridge (after the now familiar Trenton Bridge Lobster Pound). Route 230 traces the

➡ Side Trip to Sunshine Island

Just after the town office in Deer Isle Village is Sunshine Road. A left onto Sunshine Road brings you to Mountainville and Sunshine Island via a couple more causeways. Sunshine Road fans out at the last island to **Eaton's Pier** (sign on road), a lobster pound restaurant, in case you've worked up an appetite.

Returning westward on Sunshine Road, follow signs to the Haystack Mountain School of Crafts. A visitor's center, open during the summer, displays work by artists and artisans who come from across the nation. Turn around and return via Sunshine Road to Route 15 south for Stonington. ∎

east side of Union River Bay with glimpses of the shore. The road is rural, well conditioned, and avoids the more heavily traveled Route 3. A good riding road!

Entering Ellsworth (to be discussed later), take two quick lefts, the first at Route 1 and the second left at Route 172. You barely touch the town before slipping down the west side of the bay to the small village of Surry. Route 176 continues along the edge of the Blue Hill Peninsula through East Blue Hill to Blue Hill. Five routes intersect at various junctions within the town of Blue Hill. Don't get impatient; wait until you see the junction of Route 172 south (the signs also read SOUTH BLUE HILL/BLUE HILL FALLS).

The Blue Hill Fair is more than 100 years old. This old-fashioned country fair offers all of the good things that old-timers remember and all the new things that the young find exciting. Every Labor Day weekend, the fairgrounds just east of the village come alive with activity. The fair inspired E. B. White's famous children's book, *Charlotte's Web*.

Farther south on Route 175 is the village of Brooklin and Naskeag Road. A small detour down the Naskeag Road brings you to a scenic point and harbor looping back to Route 175. The **Brooklin General Store** at the intersection of Route 175 and Naskeag Road has good coffee and company.

Route 175 wraps around the Benjamin River in Sedgwick, through Sargentville, and hooks inland at the intersection of Route 15. Take Route 15 south, crossing Eggemoggin Reach via a large suspension bridge, to the series of islands beginning with Little Deer Isle. This will add the unique experience of causeway driving to your road repertoire. These narrow roadways sitting on top of the ocean leave you totally at the mercy of the weather. The first time I crossed this set of causeways, "the breeze she be ablowin'," and the roads were wet with ocean spray, the waters lapping the edge of the road-

In Castine Harbor, the State of Maine, *Maine Maritime Academy's training vessel, is open for tours when in port. If you're in port, go for it!*

way. The channels between the islands focus the wind across the causeways and the crosswinds created by the island formation are strong and unpredictable. The best way to judge the crosswinds is to watch the surface of the ocean as you approach the causeways.

(See Side Trip to Sunshine Island)

The largest village on the island, Stonington is still a working fishing harbor that depends on lobstering, scallop dragging, and boat building for its livelihood. There is a smattering of tourist stuff like galleries, inns, and restaurants. West Main Street splits off from Route 15A for a little coastal run before rejoining 15A at Burnt Cove. It returns to Route 15 north at Deer Isle Village and takes you and your scooter back to the mainland.

Route 15 north to Route 175 north to Route 199 south rounds Northern Bay, bringing you to Castine. Signs for Castine appear on Route 199.

Castine, a historic site on the National Register, is located at the mouth of the Penobscot River. Originally a trading post established by the Plymouth Pilgrims, it is the site of the worst U.S. Naval defeat in history. Trying to regain Castine from the British by sea in 1779, the colonists lost 40 ships.

Maybe that's why the Maine Maritime Academy is located here. The **State of Maine training vessel** is open for half-hour tours when in port. In

A little retribution for Judge Buck ordering someone a "flaming stake."

the harbor, small lobster boats bob next to vacationers' yachts and larger commercial ships.

Routes 166A and 175 north give you views all along the coastline up to Route 1 in Orland. In Bucksport, just before the Waldo-Hancock suspension bridge where Route 1 crosses the Penobscot River, is the cemetery and headstone of Old Judge Buck. It seems that long ago, in the early 1700s, Buck sentenced a woman to be burned for witchcraft. Her curse at the burning was "so long my curse be upon thee and my sign upon thy tombstone." As the flames consumed her, a leg rolled out of the fire. As soon as Judge Buck's tombstone was set in place the leg appeared on it.

Route 1 north to Ellsworth is a straight shot at highway speed for 20 miles. If you can't make it back to the lobster pounds on Route 3 or you need a change of pace, there are two restaurants I recommend in Ellsworth. The first is **Maidee's International Restaurant** on Main Street, a Chinese restaurant open Wednesday through Saturday. The second is **Jasper's Restaurant** on Route 1. If you're tired of the "same old" boiled lobster, Jasper's serves lobster 10 ways: stewed, baked, stuffed, newburg, alfredo, salad, casserole . . .

Places of Interest

Bar Harbor

Bar Harbor Internet Café, 27 Cottage Street. Phone 207-288-3509. This cafe opened originally in 1986 as an upscale restaurant, The Opera House, but changed to its present form in 1991, retaining the Opera House theme and furnishings. The cafe provides access to black and white and color printers and two dozen computers; it also has connections available for your own laptop, pda, etc. Good coffee drinks and home-baked pastries. $

Jordan's Restaurant, 60 Cottage Street. Phone 207-288-3586. Daily 6:30 a.m. to 2:00 p.m. Open May to October. Good food at good prices. The natives eat here. $$

Lompoc Cafe, 36 Rodick Street. Phone 207-288-9392. Open daily 3:00 p.m. to 1:00 a.m. Open end of May to mid-October. Good desserts, coffee, and microbrewery. Entertainment at 9:00 p.m. $$

The Unusual Cabaret, 14-1/2 Mt. Desert Street. Phone 207-288-3306. Opens 6:00 p.m. with singing wait staff, shows starting at 9:00 p.m. Open from mid-May to mid-October. $8 for entrees, $6 for theater. $$

Deer Isle

Eaton's Pier, Sunshine Road. Phone 207-348-2489. Daily 11:00 a.m. to 7:00 p.m. Closed Sundays. Mid-May to October. $$

Ellsworth

Maidee's International Restaurant, 156 Main Street. Phone 207-667-6554. Open Tuesday through Saturday 4:00 p.m. to 10:00 p.m. Chinese food. $$

Jasper's Restaurant & Motel, 200 High Street (Route 1). Phone 207-667-5318. "The King of Seafood." $$

Riverside Café, Main Street. Phone 207-667-7220. Open daily for breakfast and lunch. Fresh baked pastries, and you can help yourself to coffee while waiting for a table. $$

Mt. Desert Island

Acadia National Park, Visitor Center, Hulls Cove. Phone 207-288-3338. The park is open year-round, the visitor center from

May to October. $10 for a seven day pass. Mailing address for information is P.O. Box 117, Bar Harbor, 04609.

Jordan Pond House, Park Loop Road. Phone 207-276-3316. Daily 11:30 a.m. to 8:00 p.m. Open May through October. Afternoon tea on the lawn. $$$

Mt. Desert Campground, Route 198. Phone 207-244-3710. www.mountdesertcampground.com. Monday, Tuesday, Thursday 8:30 a.m. to noon; Open from June to September. 175 sites, water view upon request, reservations recommended. $24–$39.

Northeast Harbor

The Colonel's Restaurant, Main Street. Phone 207-276-5147. Daily 6:30 a.m. to 8:00 p.m. Open year-round. Fresh fish sandwiches and desserts. $$

Asticou Azalea Garden, intersection of Rte 3 and Rte 198, Northeast Harbor. Open daylight hours from May 1 through October 31.

Sullivan

Ruth & Wimpy's Kitchen, Route 1. Phone 207-422-3643. Open daily 11:00 a.m. to 10:00 p.m. Closing time varies. May to October. $$

Trenton

Trenton Bridge Lobster Pound, Route 3, Trenton. Phone 207-667-2977. Daily 10:00 a.m. to 9:00 p.m. Open May to mid-October. The best lobster. $$

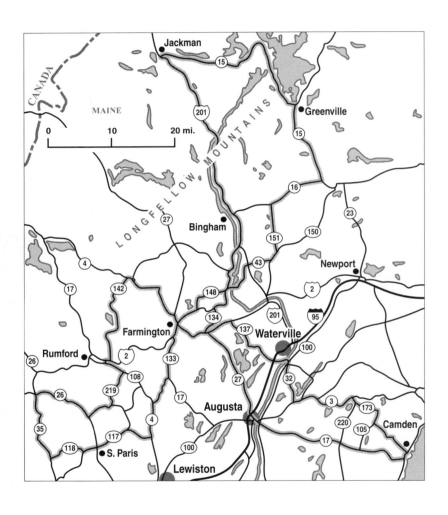

Sweeping Central Maine

Just the mention of Maine evokes images of lobster boats, lighthouses, and a rocky coastline, but this is just a small portion of the Pine Tree State. Riding inland from the coast you discover beautiful small villages, picturesque lakes, and old mill towns. Still farther north, riders encounter the very edge of civilization and the great northern wilderness.

Farmington, the hub city for central Maine, is also one of the main campuses for the University of Maine. The vitality inherent in all college towns means plenty of good food, specialty shops, and things to do. **Twice Read Books** is one of the finest used book shops in Maine. **Reny's Department Store** is the place to pick up MyCoal heat pads for your boots, heavier socks, or whatever else you need for summer camping or chilly fall weather. All in

Maine's rural roads twist through woods, around spectacular lakes, alongside rivers, and over mountains.

all, it's a particularly nice place to begin or end a day of touring the countryside of central Maine.

More importantly, it's a crossroads with multiple routes spanning out in four directions. If you're not camping, stay at the **Farmington Motel,** a 1950s vintage establishment that allows your bike to be parked outside the door. Take a load off fanny, and sit in a chair on the front walkway to enjoy the evening air.

Farmington lends itself to three day-trips in central Maine, going through very different regions: the northern woods and lakes; cities and towns along the coast and major rivers; and the small towns and rural countryside of the western hills. My favorite is the western mountain region, but which you

A view up Main Street in downtown Farmington. Being a college town, there are quite a few hotels, restaurants and stores to provision your journeys.

They may look docile and slow, but don't be deceived. Moose can move very quickly, and they do not back down if they feel threatened.

choose depends upon time of year and personal preferences. Most of these rural roads are relatively free of traffic; the scenery, especially during foliage season, is glorious.

Early morning rides can be quite chilly in Maine during foliage season, and sometimes even in August. In some ways it's the best time to camp in the Maine woods, since the arrival of frost eliminates the mosquitos and black flies, which can turn an otherwise enjoyable tour into hell on earth. Two additional cautions about traveling in northern Maine: top the fuel tank often, and take the signs warning of moose very, very seriously. Moose are not mice.

Trip 5 Western Mountains Loop

Distance *166 miles*

Highlights *Country roads, small lakes, and rolling hills coupled with delightful small towns make this loop one of the most pleasant in the Pine Tree State.*

The Route from Farmington

0.0 From downtown Farmington, continue on Route 4 south (Main Street)

0.6 Turn right onto Route 2 west

3.6 Turn left onto Route 133 south

Mt. Blue is a popular ride for motorcyclists all during the summer, but during foliage season there often seems to be as many bikes as cars on Route 142.

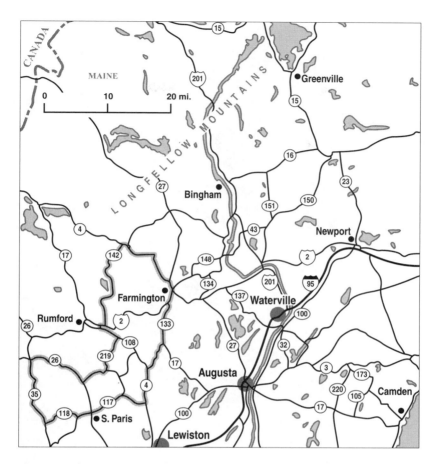

14.7 At Livermore Falls, continue on Church Street

14.9 Turn right onto Route 17, follow signs TO ROUTE 4

15.0 Turn left onto Route 4 south

32.7 Turn right onto Route 117 south

49.3 At South Paris, bear right on Route 117 south

49.7 Turn left onto Routes 117 south/26 west

50.9 At Norway, continue west on Route 117

53.4 At junction of Routes 117 and 118, continue on Route 118 west

59.3 At East Waterford, turn left onto Route 37 south

62.2 At Waterford, turn right onto Route 35 north

67.9 At Lynchville, bear right onto Routes 35 north/5 north

Perham's of West Paris is the most famous of all gem and mineral shops in the eastern United States. It's worth a stop to gaze at the fabulous specimens on display in the store.

74.4   Where Routes 35 and 5 divide, continue on Route 5 north

81.2   At Bethel, turn right onto Route 26 east

81.6   Turn left and continue on Route 26 east

97.1   At West Paris, turn left onto Route 219 north

105.0   At Sumner, bear left onto Greenwood Road

106.4   Turn right onto Labrador Pond Road, turning left at the next intersection

108.1   Continue straight onto Greenwood Road again

111.5   Turn right onto Worthley Road

115.1   At East Peru, turn left onto Route 108 west

120.1 At Dixfield, turn right onto Hammonds Road and cross the bridge

120.5 Turn right onto Route 2 east

120.8 Turn left onto Route 142

146.8 Near Phillips, turn right onto Routes 142 and 4 south

147.6 Bear right and conitnue on Route 4 south

165.9 Back in downtown Farmington

I suggest beginning the day by cruising down the four lanes of combined Routes 4 and 2 just late enough to avoid morning commuters, but early enough to miss shoppers going to the plaza, Wal-Mart, and other stores along the strip. Of course, there are several restaurants to consider stopping at for breakfast before making the turn onto Route 133 south. Route 133 defines a country touring road: silky smooth, winding through woods, past homes and small farms all the way to Livermore Falls.

It's easy to miss the turn to Route 4 in downtown Livermore Falls. Just as you begin to see the downtown commercial district you want to bear right (almost straight), turn right, and then cross the bridge over the Androscoggin River. Route 4 is a primary commercial highway leading south to Auburn and Lewiston. There's plenty of truck traffic coming and going to these cit-

The Sunday River Brewing Company, named for one of the largest ski resorts and just north of Bethel, makes a popular draft.

ies, but before reaching them you turn west in Turner onto Route 117, ride past the post office, and continue on to South Paris. Say *oui* to this pleasant rural road.

The short stretch of combined Routes 117 and 26 from South Paris to Norway turns out to be a strip development, but it quickly gives way to the old downtown, which I found to be more my style. Just west of town, and only four miles after riding down the hill into South Paris, you'll discover beautiful Pennesseewassee Lake. The roadside pulloff for the scenic area is paved, has picnic tables and a small pavilion, and is the perfect place for a group to stop. Continue straight on Route 118 for another 6 miles before making an unscheduled left turn onto Route 37 (Waterford Road).

Another beautiful spot alongside the road. For those who like to take photographs, the Western Mountain Loop offers numerous wonderful opportunities.

Beautiful Pennesseewassee Lake in Norway is a mouthful to pronounce, but easy to enjoy. A turnoff with picnic tables under a roofed pavilion is located just across the road from the lake.

After glimpsing a pond through the trees, slow down to about 45 mph and begin looking for a turnoff. Discovering such, park by a line of boulders placed to prevent cars and trucks from driving onto the wide sandy cove beach. The map indicates that this is McWain Pond. Setting up my tripod and camera, listening to the loons calling back and forth, their bark rolling across the still water, I intended to simply stop and take a few pictures. This place was so enchanting to me, I ended up catching rays on one of the large rocks, making a picnic, and watching a couple of loons dive for fish. Unscheduled changes and stops often lead to wonderful discoveries and experiences. I often find it difficult simply to follow an established route—even when I plan it!

When reaching Keoka Lake, catch Route 35 north to Lynchville where Route 5N merges. When Route 35 makes a right turn in Town House, you can elect to continue straight on Route 5, which I recommend, or remain on Route 35. Both lead to Bethel, where you turn onto Route 26.

If you have a passion for jewelry make an effort to stop at Mt. Mann on Main Street in Bethel where the proprietor, Jim Mann, mines, cuts, and sets his own gemstones. **Café di Cocoa** on Main Street in Bethel is a great place to stop for lunch, especially if you enjoy vegan and vegetarian dishes.

Maine is noted for it's tourmaline gemstones. These were mined at Black Mountain.

Oxford County is one of the world's richest sources of some types of minerals, and the most famous rock shop in the eastern United States, **Perham's of West Paris,** is situated at the intersection of Routes 26 and 219. This store offers the largest selection of rockhound and lapidary supplies in New England and displays world-famous mineral specimens in its museum. Visitors can purchase books, gemstones, jewelry, crystals, and rocks from around the world. It's also the place to obtain directions to various mines in the area, including those owned by Perham's. The rock garden out front exhibits specimens of beryl, black tourmaline, lepidolite, quartz, and other minerals mined in the local area.

Just past West Sumner turn left. A sign reads TO ROUTE 108; follow this local road through Sumner and past Worthley Pond. (My map failed to provide details of these narrow rural roads and only later I learned that my chosen route had a succession of names: Labrador Pond Road, Greenwood Road, Mud Pond Road, and Worthley Road. The joy of touring often comes from navigation by dead reckoning.)

Route 108 leads to the bridge over the Androscoggin River and Route 2 east. While tanking up with fuel at the junction in Dixfield, I saw a succession of motorcycles coming down or going up Route 142. Always a good sign for a great touring road and on this particular day it proved to be especially true. The next eleven miles gradually brought me to a higher elevation and into Mt. Blue State Park where the brilliant fall colors were approaching their peak. There's nothing quite like riding through a forest where the foliage has been transformed from green to fluorescent reds, orange, and yellow. From the beautiful little village of Weld, continue riding north through a landscape that could have been likened to an Impressionist painting. It was foliage touring at its best.

On the outskirts of the village of Phillips, Routes 142 and 4 divide and whether you continue on Route 4 or 149 is unimportant since they run in parallel down the valley with the Sandy River twisting back and forth between them. Both are great roads for cruising on a sunny afternoon (for all you Young Rascals fans). Two miles from downtown Route 27 junctions with 4 opposite the **Sawatdee Thai** restaurant and brings you back home.

Trip 6   Edge of Wilderness Loop

Distance *229 miles*

Highlights *One of the most scenic roads in Maine (Route 201) and many miles on remote roads along the edge of the Maine wilderness*

The Route from Farmington

0.0 From downtown Farmington, continue on Route 43 east (Allens Mills Road)

6.5 Turn left onto Route 148 north

18.2 At Anson, turn left on Routes 148 north/43 west

19.7 At Madison, continue straight on Routes 201A north/8

31.5 Turn right and continue on Route 201A

32.7 At Solon, turn left onto Route 201 north

90.2 At Jackman, turn right onto Routes 6 south/15 east

160.3 At Abbot Village, turn right onto Route 16 west

175.0 At Mayfield Corner, turn left onto Route 151 south

In the wilderness of northern Maine the pontoon plane becomes a preferred mode of travel. Here in Greenville you can charter one of these planes to take you to your back-country campsite.

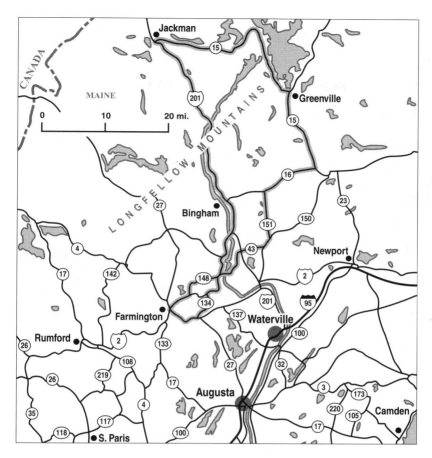

188.2 At Athens, turn right onto Route 43 west

190.0 At Cass Corner, bear right and continue on Route 43 west

195.8 Bear left and proceed diagonally across Route 201

203.0 At Madison, turn right onto Routes 43 west/148 south

203.5 Turn left and continue on routes 43 west/148 south

205.0 Bear left (actually a 90-degree corner) and continue on Route 43 west

212.2 At Anson, where Routes 43 and 134 split, turn left onto Route 134 south

220.3 At New Sharon, turn right onto Routes 2 west/27 north

227.2 At Farmington, bear right and continue on Route 27 north

228.7 End of tour in downtown Farmington

The north end of Wyman Lake is accessible from the boat dock located between Moscow and Cartunk on Route 201.

Traveling on Route 43 east of Farmington the landscape seems more appropriate for Vermont. Many of the local roads in northern Maine are crowned by logging trucks much like old wagon trails. Also, shoulders of most highways are of soft gravel which, if ridden on, give you those front-wheel wobblies.

Fog, a reality in New England river valleys during the first cold autumn mornings, creates a ethereal quality to the landscape. This was certainly true for my ride along the Kennebec River from Anson to Solon. Electrically heated gear and heavy gloves are necessities for fall foliage riding—especially in Maine!

Route 201 is designated a National Scenic Byway and riding it will feel like a national holiday. Stop in Bingham to top off the fuel tank. The many miles of solitude also means few opportunities to gas up. Besides, on a morning when the temperature hovers just above freezing, a cup of java is almost as essential for the rider as gasoline is for the bike.

Wyman Lake is a reservoir on the Kennebec River created by the dam at Moscow. It's a beautiful stretch of highway with curves and scenic pulloffs that overlook the reservoir. The northern stretch of this river above the lake is famous for its white water rafting, and many tour operators offer a wild ride down Class IV rapids. It's also a mountain region with a multitude of hiking trails leading off into the remote wilderness. Route 201 in conjunction with combined Routes 6 and 15 forms the demarcation line between civilization and the remote wilderness heaven of northern Maine.

When Route 201 leaves the river just above the Forks, the road begins a long climb into the mountains. Here, signs of moose (mud wallows) and signs warning of moose (big yellow signs with flashing yellow lights) become more frequent alongside the highway. Since the average adult moose outweighs a rider and heavily laden motorcycle by about five hundred pounds, pay attention to the signs and constantly scan left and right ready for an ambush.

Jackson is a small village, but a major outpost for those venturing into the backcountry. The turn onto combined Routes 6 and 15 is about a half-mile south of the village, but if you didn't top your fuel tank in Bingham, you had better consider riding into Jackman before continuing because there are only two or three small one-pump gas stations for the next fifty miles.

The vast lands of northern Maine are primarily owned by the paper companies, and the softwoods logged here are hauled south to the pulp mills in towns like Livermore and Rumford. Despite the meager "beauty strip" left along the road, the effects of clear cutting are evident and the height of the scrub brush is an indication of how long ago the logging took place. Signs for guide services are frequent as you ride down the southern sides of Long

Pond and Brassua Lake. Moosehead Lake is one of the largest in New England and one of the least populated. I tried to find a vantage point from which to photograph the dramatic cliff face on Mt. Kineo, an island in Moosehead Lake just north of the small village of Rockwood. This far north, trees form an important barrier that prevents drifting snow from blocking the roads during the winter and the highway department isn't about to remove them simply to provide a view for tourists.

Greenville is located at the southern end of Moosehead Lake, and besides being the region's service provider, it's a thriving summer tourist town. I stopped and enjoyed my picnic lunch at the public park and boat dock, but there are numerous restaurants, cafes, and a couple of grocery stores in the village. If you're up for a different type of touring, stop at the **Moosehead Marine Museum** and take a look at the *Katahdin,* a former steamship now converted to diesel-powered engines. Several tours of Moosehead Lake are offered, but even the shortest of them would take up the remainder of the day, so you decide.

Long stretches of open highway beckon riders to explore northern Maine.

The heights before Jackman afford a splendid panoramic view of Attean Lake and Maine's northwestern wilderness.

In Abbot Village, turn right onto Route 16 west and enjoy a pleasant ride through shaded woods. Mayfield Corners is simply a name on a map where Route 151 junctions with Route 16. Not a building is to be seen, but in the middle of the nineteenth century, places like this were thriving small communities that dwindled in population and finally were abandoned as New Englanders heeded Horace Greeley's admonishment to "go West young man."

Pick up Route 43 west by the Athens General Store. It leads you into Madison and across the bridge into Anson. For 1.5 miles you'll be back on pavement covered during the morning. Route 43 west takes you directly back to Farmington.

The return to Farmington on combined Routes 2 west and 27 north is smooth as silk, and a rider can look around and enjoy the views of rolling farmland as the late afternoon sun throws long shadows across the landscape

Trip 7 Central Maine Loop

Distance *173 miles.*

Highlights *Riding on beautiful roads through the countryside, this trip also pays a visit to downtown Augusta and the fringes of Waterville, two of Maine's most popular, and scenic, coastal towns.*

The Route from Farmington

0.0 Proceed south on Route 27

1.5 Bear left onto Routes 27 south/2 east

10.0 At New Sharon, turn right and continue on Route 27 south

36.6 In Augusta, turn left onto Bridge Street

37.0 Bear right onto Routes 9/17 south

There was a moose here just a couple of minutes ago. It's amazing how quickly an animal weighing up to 1,800 pounds and supporting antlers spanning five feet can just melt into the dense scrub woods. They can appear just as quickly.

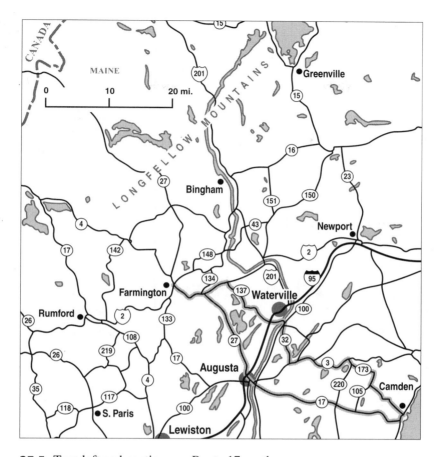

37.5 Turn left and continue on Route 17 south

73.0 At West Rockport, turn left onto Route 90 east

75.8 In Rockport, proceed straight across Route 1 onto West Street

76.0 Turn left onto Pascals Street

76.4 Turn left onto Union Street

77.9 In Camden, turn right onto Route 1 north

78.1 Turn left onto Route 105 north

83.4 At Hope, Maine, bear left and continue on Route 105 north

89.4 Turn right onto Route 131 north

97.1 At Morrill, turn left onto Route 3 south

122.6 Continue straight through on Routes 3/0/32/202

123.9 At South China, turn right onto Route 32 west

Augusta, the capitol of Maine, is an appealing small city with a large student population, and all the necessities to stock up.

135.7 At Waterville, turn left onto Route 137 north

135.8 Turn right onto Routes 137 north/201 north

136.6 Turn left across the bridge

136.8 Continue on Route 137 north

137.2 Continue on Route 137 north/11 south

141.4 At Oakland, proceed straight onto Dunn Street, which becomes West Pleasant Street

141.8 Continue onto Route 137 north

148.3 Turn right onto Route 137 north/8

151.7 At Smithfield, bear left and continue on Route 137 north

156.3 Turn left onto Route 2 west

163.0 At New Sharon, Route 27 joins Route 2

171.0 At Farmington, bear right onto Route 27 north

172.5 Back in downtown Farmington

Head out of town going east to New Sharon, turn right, and continue south on Route 27 to Augusta. The ride through the wooded countryside and down the narrow natural causeway that separates Long Pond from Great Pond brings you to the enchanting village of Belgrade Lakes. While still on the outskirts of Augusta the highway merges with Routes 8 and 11 and the traffic becomes heavier as commuters head into the city.

I suggest stopping at the Irving service station just before Exit 31 of Interstate 95. It's a busy place with a wide selection of coffee and fresh-made pastries. The concrete picnic tables and a safe place to park the bike make it an ideal place to fortify yourself with a continental-style breakfast before tackling Maine's capitol city.

Take the turn to Bridge Street, leading down the hill to downtown Augusta. If you continue straight on State Street until reaching the rotary, you'll then cross Memorial Bridge, which arches over the narrow valley and Kennebec River. This proves not to be a major problem as it leads to a second rotary and down the hill, across the old bridge, and into the downtown area.

Fort Western was erected by Dutch traders in 1754 and used as a trading post and fort until 1810. Although the blockhouse and stockade are modern reconstructions, the main fort (barracks and store) is original and one of the oldest surviving wooden forts in New England. Situated in the middle of this city its rustic appearance is in marked contrast to the buildings glimpsed beyond the stockade. From downtown, or the fort, simply ride up the hill to the rotary, bear left (a left *turn* takes you over the Memorial Bridge), and follow Route 17 out of the city.

Fort Western in Augusta is one of the oldest original wooden forts in the United States.

That special whatchamacallit can be found at Dale Weaver's if you can spend the time to search for it.

Fifteen miles from Augusta, I spied a treasure trove, but couldn't tell whether it was a junkyard or perpetual yard sale. The owner arrived as I was dismounting to take a closer look, and while Dale Weaver went about his morning routine of opening up the barn, I eased along the narrow pathways that meandered through the sea of junk. In reality it was all quite organized, but with so much stuff that sharp eyes were required to find the rare treasures hidden beneath things. Hubcaps, road signs, empty beer kegs, glassware, books, vinyl truck-bed liners, all sorts of great plumbing fixtures, garden tools, the kitchen sink (and ones for bathroom, laundry, garage, and laboratory), fishing tackle, old-fashioned irons, door knobs, storm windows, outboard motors, and much more stretched out on all sides of me. It was all here, even a Yamaha 250 and a fancy top case with a Honda almost buried beneath it. Strolling past a brass-plated bed frame, several water fountains, a stack of roof vents, a couple of hand trucks, and several B-B-Q grills, I discovered a Green River free-standing shop vise with a foot lever. It was a good thing I was riding a fully-loaded motorcycle because I discovered numerous things that otherwise would have been hauled home.

Route 1 north leads directly into downtown Camden, but I suggest continuing straight to Rockport Harbor. Turn off Pascals Street and venture down to the boat dock to check out the wooden sailing ships moored in this sheltered harbor. The *Lynx* is a two-masted, square-top-sail schooner that was launched in the year 2000, but which was based upon a ship by the same name that had been constructed in Maryland in 1812. The *Lynx,* outfitted in historic detail including bronze guns and stands of small arms, is not the only wooden sailing schooner in the harbor. Many of these others can be chartered for the day and some even offer short scheduled tours. From the harbor simply continue to Camden on Union Street passing under the Camden-Rockport Arch, a portal marking the boundary of and cooperation between the two towns.

Camden is a culturally rich town and has one of the highest densities of B&B inns in the state. As a town popular with summer tourists, parking can be a problem, even for a motorcycle. There are a number of companies offering boat charters should you decide to change your mode of travel for a few hours, whether that be on a historic schooner or a working lobster boat. Camden and Rockport also offer everything from fast food to gourmet dining, but you probably would like to know where to go for lobster. I suggest calling **Captain Andy's** and having your lobster lunch delivered to you at the harbor park or town landing and making a picnic of it. Another option would be the **Village Restaurant** on Main Street.

The Camden Arch on Union Street represents the cooperation between the towns of Rockport and Camden.

Unique 1 on Bayview Street sells woolen clothing made in Maine and the goldsmiths at **Etienne Fine Jewelry** on Main Street are internationally recognized. There are also antique shops, art galleries, and bookstores. It's very easy to spend two or three enjoyable hours in Camden before heading inland once again.

About fourteen miles outside of Camden and just before the town of Hope, I pulled over to watch Ron Russell carve a totem pole. He was making it for a neighbor, chiseling figures into the large trunk of a softwood tree. He took a break and showed me a couple of his completed projects and we fell into easy conversation. Too soon I had to mount up and continue on my way.

You need to choose whether to ride north along the west side of China Lake (Route 32), or along the more scenic eastern shore (Route 202), since both lead to Route 137 north and into Waterville. The mills powered by the Kennebec and Sebasticook rivers made Waterville a prosperous nineteenth-century industrial center, but after the beauty of Augusta and vitality of Camden it may seem a bit drab. Afternoon traffic can be a bit intense in this small city and you might be more interested in reaching the open coun-

Ron Russell of Hope, Maine, is a noted local carver. When I met him he was chiseling images on a totem pole designed for a neighbor.

Rockport Harbor is internationally known for its wooden sailing ships. Some, like the
Lynx, *are patterned after historical sailing ships from the age before steam power.*

tryside than touring this historic mill town. Fortunately, I ran into Paul
Shorette, a local rider who told me about the shortcut (Dunn and West Pleasant streets) through Oakland. This route will quickly get you out of the city
and back into the Belgrade Lakes Region.

Bear to the left by the convenience store in Smithfield and ride along the
shore of North Pond to East Mercier. Once again, Route 2 west becomes a
pleasant late afternoon ride as you jaunt back to Farmington for supper.

Places of Interest

Greenville

Moosehead Marine Museum, P.O. Box 1151, Greenville 04441. 207-695-2716. This is an essential stop for the rider who is fascinated by steam engines or steamboats. *The Katahdin* is the last of the steamboats (although it has been converted to diesel power) that once plied this lake. Three tours of Moosehead Lake, ranging from two-and-a-half hours to all day, are offered. Call for details and prices.

Farmington

Twice Read Books on Main Street feels more like a library than a store and contains a vast collection of reference books and even some rarities.

Narrow Gauge Brewing Company and the **Granary Brew Pub & Restaurant,** 147 Pleasant Street. Phone 207-779-0710. www.granary-boilerroom.com. Of course you have to try the local brew when exploring a new area! Located near the cinema you can catch a brew and then enjoy a movie before riding back to your hotel.

Sawatdee Thai, the junction of Route 43 at Route 149, Farmington. Real Thai food made using all fresh ingredients, this restaurant was a surprise find and was so good I returned a second night just to indulge myself. $$

Soups For You, Broadway, Farmington. Wrapped sandwiches, excellent soups, Italian coffee, and a great local college hangout. If you want to bring a picnic lunch on your ride, which is advisable for the northern routes, the wrap sandwiches from this small college restaurant are an excellent choice. $

R.H. Renny, Inc., 200 Broadway. Phone 207-778-4631. A great locally owned department store selling all sorts of things including clothing. I purchased extra socks with a pocket in the toes for biodegradable heating pads, which made my rides much more pleasant. Independent department stores are becoming a rarity in this age of chain stores and this locally owned business is a gem.

Twin Pond Motel & Campground, 574 Wilton Road (Route 2). Phone 800-452-4977. www.twinpond.com. One of the few campgrounds near Farmington, this one offers convenient location and surprisingly little noise from the highway.

Trees everywhere. Fall foliage is the most interesting time to tour the north woods.

Farmington Motel, 489 Farmington Falls Road (Route 2 and 27). Phone 207-778-4680. I recommend this motel highly. One of the old '50s establishments. Park your bike in front of your room and sit in chairs on the covered walkway outside of your room on hot summer evenings. The motel sits back from the road and rolling fields stretch out behind it.

Gifford's Famous Ice Cream, 293 Main Street. Phone 207-778-3617. Excellent premium ice cream, not as famous as Ben & Jerry's, but every bit as good.

West Paris

Perham's of West Paris. Phone 207-674-2341. The best rock shop in the East, located in the heart of one of the world's richest regions for gems and minerals. Tour their museum and gift shop. Better yet, scrap the tour and head out to one of five Perham-owned mines to try your own luck.

Augusta

Fort Western, downtown Augusta. Phone 207-626-2385. It's difficult not to notice a stockaded frontier fort strategically placed above the river in the center of Maine's capitol city. Take a few minutes to tour this wooden fort—there are precious few original wooden forts that survive today.

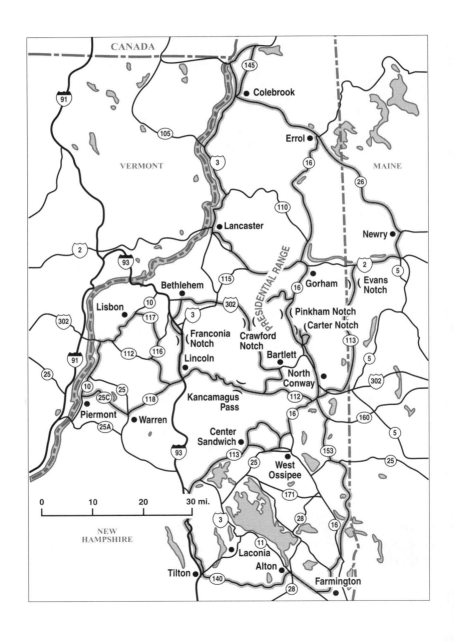

Cutting White Mountain Notches

The White Mountains are located in the upper half of New Hampshire, bordering the Connecticut River and Vermont to the west and a small portion of Maine to the east. One third of New Hampshire is over 2,000 feet in elevation, and 84 percent, including the 1,100-square-mile White Mountain National Forest, is wooded. You will notice that the Appalachian Trail, a 2,200 mile footpath from Georgia to Maine, crosses the road many times as it traverses the Presidential Range, which is considered the most challenging hiking of the entire route.

Here you will find some of the most dramatic mountain scenery in the northeast. New Hampshire is the most mountainous of the New England states. In fact, Mt. Washington is the highest peak in the Northeast (elevation 6,288 feet). There are 12 notches in the White Mountains, 11 in New Hampshire and the twelfth, Grafton Notch, in Maine. In Yankee parlance, a "notch" would be what everyone else refers to as a pass through the mountains. The early New Englanders likened these steep, rugged granite cuts to the sort of notches a woodsman's axe made in the logs he meant to use for building a cabin, and the term has stuck (or is it struck). Breathtaking in their

The spectacular Mt. Washington Valley unfolds from the summit of Mt. Washington.

The Presidential Range seen from Mt. Washington is reflected in the sign and reality. On a clear day, you can see several states, and Canada.

grandeur, dramatic to drive, the notches are blessed with a variety of good roads ranging from two-lane highways to narrow locals with more curves than a snake's back.

There are many places of all comfort levels to choose from in the region. The Conway area is quite a resort town, catering to both outdoor recreation and outlet shopping. It's former role harkens back to the days of New England poets like Thoreau and Hawthorne who spent time here enjoying the natural beauty of the mountains. During the 1930s and '40s, ski trains from Boston delivered weekend warriors to the large hotels that catered to the seasonal trade.

In more recent years, the town of North Conway has become defined instead by the many outlet stores now located here; New Hampshire has no sales tax, making it a tempting destination for a motivated bargain hunter. Consequently, Route 16 through "the Strip" harbors more traffic and hassle than the average motorcyclist would enjoy and is probably best avoided by using the local's "North-South" road one block to the east. The Village itself is not wholly without charm, however, and there are many good restaurants, several movie theaters, and every other amenity you might be searching for, including several motorcycle dealerships. It is also home to **Whitehorse Press,** publisher of books and a catalog for motorcycle enthusiasts.

My anchor point for the Winnipesaukee Warmup Loop and Western Notches Loop is located south of Conway on Route 16 in **White Lake State Park.** A vital safety tip: the moose population in northern New Hampshire and Maine is growing faster than the permits to trim it; there are literally hundreds of collisions each year. You will lose the war running into a moose. These animals can weigh up to a ton! Some sound advice from the local human inhabitants about the moose inhabitants: moose are nocturnal, so limit your night riding or at least lower your speed. Unlike deer, which freeze, moose put their heads down and bolt across the road once they decide to go. Moose also tend to be long-legged, so your headlight barely catches their belly hair. The best way to spot moose is to scan the road side-to-side continuously, because they do blend into their surroundings.

This bike climbed Mt. Washington. You'll feel the sense of accomplishment too. The popular "Auto Road" is open to motorcycles only when wind conditions are mild.

Trip 8   Winnipesaukee Warmup Loop

Distance   *149 miles without side trips*

Highlights   *Rural routes hugging the shores of scenic lakes, rivers, and ponds*

The Route from White Lake State Park

0 mi   From White Lake State Park, turn left onto Route 16 north

14.9   At the lights in Conway village, turn right onto Route 153 south

29.7   At junction of Route 25, turn left to follow Route 153/25

30.9   At junction, turn right to follow Route 153 south

63.6   In Farmington, turn right onto Route 75 west

64.5   Turn right onto Route 11 west

73.1   In Alton, turn left onto Route 140 west

94.6   At Tilton, turn right onto Route 132 north

New England at its finest

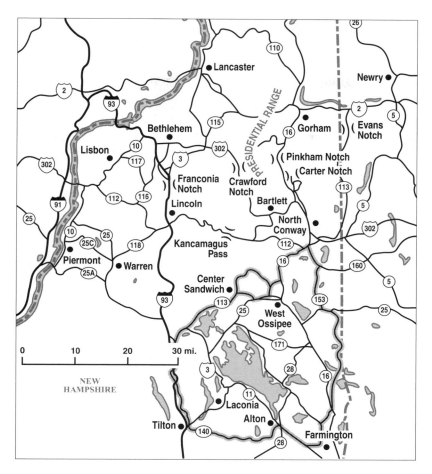

106.8 At New Hampton, follow Route 132 north through town

108.1 Where Routes 104 and 132 split, turn left to stay on Route 132

115.0 In Ashland, turn right onto Route 3 south

118.8 At Holderness, turn left onto Route 113 east

130.6 At Center Sandwich, turn left to stay on Route 113 east

134.2 At North Sandwich, turn right to stay on Route 113 east

138.1 At junction with Route 25, turn left to stay on Route 113 east

141.3 Where Routes 25 and 113 split, turn left to stay on Route 113 east

143.3 At Tamworth, turn right to stay on Route 113 east

146.2 At Chocorua, turn right onto Route 16 south

149.2 Turn right into White Lake State Park

Squam Lake was the shoot location for the film On Golden Pond. You can get homemade ice cream at the Squam Lakeside Farm, a large barn opposite the lake. I found it a good stopping place, especially for an ice cream meister like myself.

Route 16 north will take you past scenic Chocorua Lake. Mt. Chocorua dominates the area around the lake and is named after the Indian chief Chocorua who, according to popular legend, was friendly to the white settlers and befriended in particular a family named Campbell. Leaving on a hunting expedition, Chocorua left his motherless son with the Campbells for safekeeping. The Campbells, being harassed by some wolves, made a poison which Chocorua's son swallowed accidentally and died. Chocorua, on his return, could not accept the death as an accident. He killed the Campbells. Hunted by the other settlers, Chocorua was shot, climbed the mountain, and leapt to his death, cursing the white man with his final breath.

Before entering the village of Conway you'll pass **Bill's Place** restaurant owned by John and Dian Birkbeck. Bill's Place offers hearty, home-style meals at budget-friendly prices. Once a month, during the warmer months, you'll find the parking lot filled with Harleys as Bill's hosts the local HOG chapter's monthly meetings.

Route 153 is a narrow, curvy road. Although it has an occasional bumpy part, the ride generally hugs the land over hills and around the lakes. It features very little traffic and few gas stations, so be sure to top off your tank. This is a riding road with few villages to interrupt your pace, so sit back and enjoy or scoot forward and roll on. Watch the road signs to be warned of surprise 90-degree turns coming just over the crest of the small hill ahead (this happens a few times, so all the more fun). If you are tired, choose from a number of lakes to rest, the prettiest on Route 153 being Province Lake.

The small towns along Route 153 offer diner-type ambiance. The **Poor People's Pub,** in Sanbornville, is a "cheap eats" lunch and supper place, with five-dollar pitchers of cold drinks, homemade soups, desserts, and pub grub. There are always a couple of steeds parked outside.

Route 153 intersects Route 75 after crossing Route 16. Route 75 and a rather commercial Highway 11 get you from Route 153 to Route 140.

You can eat up Route 113 in Sandwich, New Hampshire.

Route 140 is a great road with little traffic and good curves where your skill determines your speed level. The driving is in the 35 to 55 mph range. This route leads eventually to Route 132, a delightful surprise that ripples and plays tag with Interstate 93. While all those cars are heading straight north, you're playing peek-a-boo with them.

Route 132 takes you past the **Tilt'n Diner,** an old-fashioned roadside diner offering good food at reasonable prices. If you're lucky enough to arrive on "cruise night," the tunes from the '50s and '60s, nostalgic décor, and classic old cars offer a little "twilight zone" experience.

Ending the rhythm of the Route 132-step when merging with Route 3, my mind was smoking and I figured, "Oh good, a chance to catch my breath." But nooo. Just before Squam Lake in Holderness, Route 113 begins. If you do want to catch your breath before leaving Holderness, be sure to stop by the **Squam Lake Natural Science Center,** located at the intersection of Routes 3 and 113. You could easily spend three to four hours exploring the self-guided trails and interactive exhibits. The Gephart Trail features live, native New Hampshire wildlife including bear, bobcats, red fox, mountain lions, river otters, deer, snakes, and more. The Mt. Fayal Trail will take you to the summit for breathtaking views of Squam Lake.

The Province Lake area is beautiful, and Route 153 which winds through this area is a popular motorcycling road.

➡ Side Trip to Route 113A

Route 113A off Route 113 at North Sandwich. Route 113A rejoins route 113.

If you still have the time or inclination to extend the ride, branch off Route 113 to Route 113A.

Route 113A is as curvy as Route 113, but is less used. The road is tighter and narrower than Route 113, a little more bumpy, too, but avoids a couple of small towns. You'll find the Hemmenway State Recreational Area along this route. There's a hiking trail leading up to the Great Hill Fire Tower. The complete hike is not recommended for those wearing motorcycle boots, but you could certainly walk down to the bridge crossing the Swift River. It's a nice spot to cool your jets with plenty of elbow room. Route 113A reconnects with Route 113 at Tamworth, N.H.   ■

Route 113 redefines the word "smooth" in the context of road feel. It might also have been the quietness created by my ears being blocked from a long twisting ascent. The climb, after leaving Squam Lake, up Route 113 east toward Mt. Chocorua is an up, down, and around love affair with the transition from lake to mountain. This road has more curves than a day's worth of hourglasses. The engineer must have been a descendant of the Sidewinder family. Speed will definitely dictate the amount of challenge this terrain has to offer. Your ability to accelerate out of and decelerate into these rapid curves smoothly and safely is a measure of your skill. Passing through Center Sandwich, N.H., on your left you'll see an earthen road that crosses Sandwich Notch. Count it as a viewing but not a crossing—this road is a challenge even for those riding dual-sport bikes. You see enough notches on this journey that sacrificing the steed on this one is unnecessary.

(See Side Trip to Route 113A)

Route 113 intersects with Route 16. At Chocorua, follow it south to home base.

Trip 9   Western Notches Loop

Distance *217 miles*

Highlights *Enjoy rural highways and ascents to river runs and famed tourist attractions. If you spend lots of time at the latter, the route can be easily shortened by about 40 miles. Notch roads are known for being twisty, up-and-down, scenic runs.*

The Route from White Lake State Park

0 mi From White Lake State Park, turn left onto Route 16 north

14.2 Near Conway, turn left onto Route 112 west (Kancamagus Highway)

26.4 Turn right onto Bear Notch Road

35.4 In Bartlett, turn left onto Route 302 west

66.5 In Bethlehem, turn left onto Route 142 south

71.8 Turn left onto Route 18 south

75.8 Turn right onto I-93/Route 3 south

Out in the rugged New Hampshire wilderness, the fabulous Mt. Washington Hotel emerges.

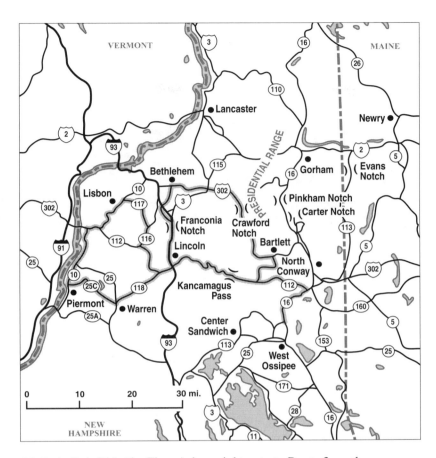

81.6 At Exit 34A (the Flume), bear right onto to Route 3 south

86.8 In North Woodstock, turn right onto Route 112 west

89.3 Turn left onto Route 118 south (Sawyer Highway)

102.2 At Warren, turn right onto Route 25 west (Moosilauke Highway)

115.8 At Piermont, turn right onto Route 10 north

124.0 Proceed straight ahead onto Route 10 north/Route 302 east

135.7 A mile or so beyond Lisbon, turn right onto Route 117 east

143.9 In Franconia, turn right onto Route 116 south

144.4 Turn right to stay on 116 south

155.6 At the junction with Route 112, turn left onto Route 112 east

202.4 Near Conway, turn right onto Route 16 south

216.6 Turn right into White Lake State Park

You can always find like-minded folk running the Kancamagus Highway (the Kanc); a bit of the Alps in New Hampshire.

This loop includes some of the best-known natural attractions in the region and the most notches crossed in the White Mountains journey. Prepare for a long day if you want to see everything, since the sights are usually crowded, although the facilities seem to manage the flow well. If necessary, you can shorten your ride by cutting off the last portion of the loop, depending on your sightseeing preferences.

If you wish to grab some food to have a picnic along the scenic Kancamagus Highway, proceed about a half a mile beyond your intended turn onto Route 112 and you will find the **Chinook Café,** known locally for its sustaining and tasty wraps—a portable feast in the making. But any time of the day, you will find wonderful fare and a cozy atmosphere; consider a dinner stop, since you will be returning to the junction of Route 112 and 16 at the end of the day. Note that their Sunday brunch is a worthy occasion.

Route 112 is the **Kancamagus Highway** (locals call it "the Kanc," pronounced like "crank" without the "r"). A nationally renowned scenic highway, the road can carry heavy tourist traffic, especially during foliage season. The route will sweep and twist as it follows the meandering Swift River. On a hot day you will see plenty of ponies parked by the road as motorcyclists stop to claim a spot of their own along the tumbling banks. In about seven miles you will pass Lower Falls, a wonderful multi-level swimming hole with deep pools and cascading waters.

While the Kanc is generally in pretty good shape, you should not expect perfection. Most of these traditional mountain roads will have flaws and bumps in the pavement and you should pay close attention to the road surface. Besides, this ride should be savored, not swilled. You will be returning this way at the end of the day.

About 13 miles up the Kancamagus is Bear Notch Road, the first notch of the loop. The nine-mile drive north on Bear Notch Road offers several overlooks with views to Crawford Notch, Mt. Washington, and the Carter Range. This is a lovely, untrafficked stretch of sun-dappled pavement overhung with trees.

Route 302 ascends to Crawford Notch with wide passing lanes, so the traffic is not a bother. As the hills rise up abruptly on either side, you can clearly see the trestles of the Conway Scenic Railroad running horizontally along the steep slopes.

As the road begins to crest, take a break at the Crawford Notch train station and Macomber Information Center. Built in 1891 as an outpost for the Maine Central Railway, the depot is now used by the Conway Scenic Railroad, which runs tours through the notch. The newly constructed **Appalachian Mountain Club Highland Center** offers rooms, meals, and other amenities to hikers—the Appalachian Trail intersects with Route 302 here, a junction that brings together people from diverse backgrounds, all sharing in the raw beauty of the area. It makes a great 20-minute people-watching break.

You'll pass many great swimming holes on your ride up the Kanc. People from all over come to appreciate this natural waterpark.

As you approach the summit of Crawford Notch, the road tends to flatten. About four miles up the road, the **Mt. Washington Hotel** comes into view: an elaborate wooden structure built in the tradition of the grand hotels popular in the early 1900s here in the White Mountains. Few others have survived over the years, some falling to fire, others to the economy. Newly refurbished, this particular place was the site of the famous 1944 Bretton Woods Economic Summit, which established the International Monetary Fund and World Bank. Feel free to park your bike and wander about, soaking up the history and luxury from the veranda.

From this spot, you can enjoy a most dramatic view of Mt. Washington, as it seems to loom over the hotel. On a clear day, you should be able to see the towers of the Observatory building, as well as the chuffing smoke of the **Cog Railway,** as it works itself up Jacob's Ladder, a stretch of track with a grade in excess of 37 percent! Built in 1869, this mountain-climbing steam locomotive was the pinnacle of engineering technology in its day. If you'd like a closer look, take a right onto Base Road just before Fabyan's, the terminus of the modern Scenic Railroad.

Before you've gone too much farther on Route 302, note that the speed limit will abruptly decrease to 30 mph and you should comply: this portion of the road is heavily patrolled, as the state police station is only a few miles away.

Oliverian Notch is one of the more obscure notches you can bag on this loop. Not much traffic here!

This is probably one of the last published photographs of the "Old Man of the Mountain." The very forces that created his visage caused him to give way in May 2003.

The ride from Route 142 to Route 18 to Interstate 93 consists of small roads with little of note. Franconia Notch Parkway holds the main events in the area for tourists. The Cannon Mountain tramway will give you unprecedented views of Franconia State Park and the rugged granite peaks for which the area is known. Also located at the base of the ski area is the **New England Ski Museum,** with rotating yearly exhibits as well as videos and a permanent display depicting the history of the industry as it evolved from barrel slats and thong bindings to the high-tech equipment used today.

The natural phenomena of the Flume and the Old Man of the Mountain are enduring tourist magnets, exploited to the hilt. They are worth going through and to; I just want to set your expectations for the six miles (Smokies are everywhere).

The **Old Man of the Mountain** is the state symbol of New Hampshire and his likeness graces many things, including the highway signs you have been following. The granite visage was formed of five separate ledges that totaled more than 40 feet in height. However, in early May, 2003, the fog lifted after several days of cold, damp weather that obscured the Old Man, and National Forest personnel were aghast to find that the Old Man was

Entering Franconia Notch State Park with Cannon Mountain ski area in the distance provides you with loads of sweepers.

gone! Millennia of hard weather had finally taken their toll and the face literally fell from the mountain. To get a good view of where it once was, you must park and walk about 1,800 feet along a broad footpath that curves around Profile Lake. You'll notice that the remaining section of Route 93/3 is a fairly claustrophobic stretch of high-speed divided highway, one lane in either direction, but it doesn't last too long.

The **Flume Gorge,** a geologic wonder, offers a spectacular walk through a natural chasm of cascading waterfalls. From this point onward, Route 3 is chockful of family attractions, resorts, cottages, and campgrounds pandering to the summer trade.

Whew! Once you make it through the Franconia Notch gauntlet, open up the throttle, accelerate out of the attractions, and head straight into the curves of our original objective. All the "100" routes (Routes 112, 116, 117, and 118) are joys to ride—twisting and turning like Chubby Checker on a cheap vibrator bed, no quarters needed! You can add two more notches to your belt along the way, too. The Oliverian Notch can be seen from Route 25 just over Lake Tarlton. Route 112 west to Route 118 south will get you there.

If you'd like to maximize your sightseeing time, shorten the trip by 38 miles by staying on Route 112 west to 302 east. Skip the 118-to-25C-to-10 loop.

You'll still find a few typical wooden bridges that span New England rivers and streams.

Route 10, like most major north-south roads, follows a river (the Connecticut). Unlike most river roads, which travel the floor of the valley, Route 10 sits high up, with gentle farmland fields flowing down to the river banks. This reminds me more of Vermont terrain than of New Hampshire; in fact, the opposite shore line is Vermont. Where Route 10 north joins Route 302 east, you start to veer away from the river.

About four miles up Route 10/302, you will run into the wide-spot-in-the-road that is the town of Bath, N.H., the Covered Bridge Capitol of New Hampshire and home of the **Brick Store,** the oldest operating general store in America, and it still manages to retain a cracker-barrel authenticity that Hollywood can't quite imitate. Original counters and glass cases display groceries and sundries, as well as their very own smoked meats and homemade fudge (free samples). A quick left behind the store has you at the threshold of the **Bath Village Bridge,** the longest covered bridge in N.H. and one of the oldest in America. Note that the weight limit for the structure is six tons, so go easy on the fudge . . .

Route 117 is a lazy road of forest and hills. When you reach the town of Sugar Hill, slow down and look for Sunset Hill Road. It doesn't matter what time of day it is; the 1,500-foot elevation atop Sugar Hill makes the view one of the sweetest. If you want to blow your budget, make reservations for the

Sunset Hill House. Its rooms overlooking the Presidential Range and its country French cuisine will provide a lifelong memory.

Just after Sunset Hill on Route 117 is **Polly's Pancake Parlor.** If, like me, you're a firm believer that breakfast is the most important meal of the day, regardless of the hour, Polly's Pancake Parlor is a must on your list if you arrive before they close. The "parlor" was built in 1830 as the carriage shed and later woodshed to the Hildex Maple Sugar Farm. During the Depression, Polly and Wilfred (Sugar Bill) Dexter began serving "all you can eat" pancakes and waffles for fifty cents. Sixty years later, the family still lives at and manages the farm and Parlor. All the mixes are made from scratch and include whole wheat, buckwheat, oatmeal, buttermilk, and cornmeal pancakes. The grains are organically grown and are stone ground by the proprietors. Their forte though are maple products, which are toppings for the fare. (Did I mention the cob-smoked bacon?)

Upon rejoining Route 117, you will merge with Route 116 south. These roads bring you straight (figuratively, not literally) back to Route 112. Route 112, west of Interstate 93, parallels the wild Ammonoosuc River and is a much less traveled road than the Kancamagus Highway, which is the east side of Route 112. The Kingsman Notch is on Route 112 heading east, just before North Woodstock, N.H.

Polly's Pancake Parlor has the absolute best pancakes and maple sugar products anywhere. Pass the syrup!

Speaking of sweet stuff, how about this view from Sugar Hill?

If you need to top off your human tank, you will find ample refreshment in the town of Lincoln. For a taste of homemade pastry and Italian treats, check out the **Wise Guy's Café** in the Mill Front Marketplace. On the left side of the plaza you'll find the **Chatroom,** a nicely appointed internet café where you can sip a fruit smoothie or a cappucino while checking your email.

When you cross Interstate 93 in the town of Lincoln, the Kancamagus begins. There are many scenic vista parking areas overlooking the Pemigewasset Wilderness, and Kancamagus Pass could be your sixth notch of the loop except for the nomenclature. Kancamagus, the grandson of Passaconoway and the nephew of Wonalancet, was the third and final sagamore of the Pennacook Confederacy. As you crest the height of land, you will be crossing from the Merrimack to the Saco River valley. A right turn onto Route 16 south will have you back at home base in less than 15 miles.

Trip 10   North Country Notches Loop

Distance *253 miles without side trips*

Highlights *This one-day ride will take you from the gentle hills of central New Hampshire to the highest point in the northeastern United States. From there you'll press on further north, past the 45th parallel into the mossy spruce forests of "moose alley" and back home again. You'll enjoy dramatic scenery, mountain climbs, sweeping river road curves, and roller-coaster hills.*

The Route from White Lake State Park

0 mi From White Lake State Park, turn left onto Route 16 north

15.0 In Conway, turn left to stay on Route 16 north

26.1 In Glen, bear right to stay on Route 16 north

The Balsams in Dixville Notch is one of the few remaining grand old resorts of the White Mountains. A cool drink and a stroll through their formal garden is a great way to break up a ride.

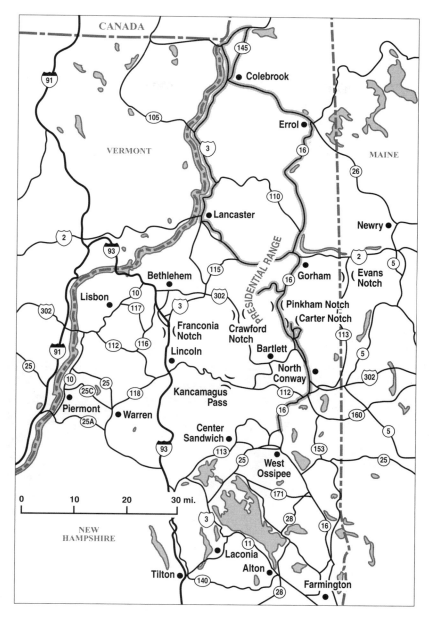

28.4 At Jackson, turn right onto Route 16A (Jackson covered bridge)

29.0 Bear right onto Route 16B

30.6 Turn left to stay on Route 16B

32.2 Turn left to stay on Route 16B (Carter Notch Road)

34.3 Turn right onto Route 16A

34.7 Turn right onto Route 16 north

46.6 Mt. Washington Auto Road side trip or proceed on Route 16 north

54.4 In Gorham, turn left onto Route 16 north/Route 2

55.8 Turn left onto Route 2 west

72.8 Near Jefferson, turn right onto the North Road

79.9 In Lancaster, turn right onto Route 3 north

80.6 Bear right to stay on Route 3 north

129.3 In Pittsburg, turn right onto Route 145 south

147.4 In Colebrook, turn left onto Route 26 east

169.0 In Errol, turn right onto Route 16 south

204.8 In Gorham, turn right to stay on Route 16 south

253.3 Turn right into White Lake State Park

Plenty of bikes climb the Auto Road. If you're in the area, and the timing is right, go for it!

Start out from White Lake State Park through North Conway on Route 16. In Glen, 26 miles north of base camp, turn right at the traffic light to remain on Route 16. Here you start to feel, not just see, the high country. Only 2.4 miles farther, turn right over the picturesque covered bridge to Jackson village. One-half mile beyond the bridge is the intersection of Routes 16A and 16B. Bear right onto Route 16B and ride up the steep hill following the Route 16B loop. You are heading into your first notch of the day, Carter Notch. The road climbs higher and higher past meadows and mountain views. Just before the Black Mountain ski area, turn sharply left to remain on Route 16B and begin your descent on the second half of the Carter Notch loop. After crossing a river at the intersection with the Carter Notch Road, turn left and return to your loop's start, the intersection of Routes 16A and 16B. You'll pass historic inns and scenic Jackson Falls as you complete the Carter Notch loop.

Turn right on Route 16A, returning to Route 16 and turn right, heading north. This section of road sweeps from side to side and climbs steadily into the White Mountain National Forest. The Presidential Range, sometimes referred to as the "Ridgepole of New England," starts to loom larger and larger off to the west.

The drama builds as you enter Pinkham Notch (add it to your collection); the full mountain range is at your feet. Mt. Washington, the highest peak in the Northeast (elevation 6,288 feet), has some of the harshest weather in North America. In fact, the highest wind ever recorded was measured at 237 mph on the summit in the 1938 hurricane. There is plant life at the summit that only thrives in arctic conditions. And . . . you can get to the summit via the Mt. Washington Auto Road.

(See Side Trip to Mt. Washington)

Rejoining Route 16 north in your invigorated state, head for the northern reaches of the White Mountains. Because of its proximity to the Appalachian Trail and the Presidential Range, Gorham, at the junction of Routes 2 and 16, is popular with hikers, bikers, and outdoor sports people. Just eight miles north of the Mt. Washington Auto Road, you can choose from a variety of motels, campgrounds, small inns, and restaurants if you want to move home base farther north.

Turn left at the intersection by the Gorham village green where Route 2 joins Route 16. At the far end of the Gorham business district, turn left or west, staying on Route 2. Just ahead on the right is Jimtown Road to **Moose Brook State Park.** Open mid-May to mid-October, Moose Brook offers camping, fishing, hiking, swimming, and showers. If you do choose to move your base camp farther north, this would be a good choice. Route 2 heading west to Jefferson, is a wide, smooth two-laner with easy passing. Seventeen

The Blessing of the Bikes at Colebrook is a yearly event in mid-June that draws a big cross-section of motorcyclists.

miles from Gorham, turn right, on the North Road. This is the first right turn after the junction of Route 116 and Route 2 on your left. This alternative to staying on Route 2 to Lancaster is more rural with less traffic and more twisties.

After seven miles on North Road, you will arrive in the town of Lancaster. This is home to the largest public event in the Great North Woods region of New Hampshire, the Lancaster Fair. Each Labor Day weekend for more than 130 years, folks have turned out at the Lancaster Fairgrounds for 65 acres of fun and food. If you timed it right, don't miss this classic New England fair. Turn right on Route 3 heading north. Route 3 is a truck route until you get above Colebrook; however, it does parallel the Connecticut River from Lancaster to its headwaters in West Stewartstown, providing valley scenery.

On Route 3, 35 miles north of Lancaster, is the **Shrine of Our Lady of Grace.** This is a large shrine depicting the birth of Christ. It is also the site of an annual blessing of motorcycle riders. Thousands of bikes gather here each year in the middle of June to be blessed. The White Mountain Riders Motorcycle Club is host to the annual gathering. As you can see from the picture, this may be the only memorial to two-wheelers. It's the only one I've seen. If you know of any others, let me know.

Return to Route 3 north after the shrine, and roll into beautiful downtown Colebrook. Eight miles north of town on Route 3, in the town of West Stewartstown, you'll find the **Spa Restaurant.** In continuous operation since 1927, this landmark has been serving excellent steaks and seafood to tourists and residents alike. Just north of the Spa is a steep hill. The top of this hill is marked as the 45th parallel (halfway between the North Pole and the equator.) You are really way up north now! Just nine miles more and you are in Pittsburg, the northernmost point on your ride. At 360 square miles, Pittsburg has the distinction of being the biggest town east of the Mississippi. If you haven't seen Bullwinkle or any of his brethren yet and want to, continue on Route 3 north past First Connecticut Lake. Locals call this road, **"Moose Alley."** Watch the marshy areas for moose, especially very early in the morning or at dusk. If you see parked cars, they are probably watching moose.

Take a hard right on Route 145 south back to Colebrook. Route 145 is one of the top roller-coaster roads in New England. The first part of this 18-mile run back to Colebrook rises and falls so quickly in places that you'll feel like a fighter pilot fighting G forces! After that section, Route 145 settles into some fine twisties. Three miles before Route 145 ends back in Colebrook, it passes Beaver Brook Falls on your left. This gorgeous spot is open to the public for viewing the impressive falls, picnicking, and general relaxing. Once back in Colebrook, turn left onto Main Street (Route 3) for 150 yards then turn left onto Route 26 heading east. Get ready for Dixville Notch and The Balsams.

Route 26 climbs east, out of Colebrook. As it does, it begins to twist, following and sometimes crossing the Mohawk River. In sharp contrast to the natural beauty, you'll soon come upon a massive collection of used heavy equipment. This is Nash Equipment Sales. Fine pre-owned bulldozers, graders, tree harvesters—you name it, you can get one here. A bit under 12 miles down Route 26, you'll come to **The Balsams.** This grand old New Hampshire resort is similar to the Mt. Washington Hotel and billed as the Switzerland of the U.S. Turn left just past Lake Gloriette and views of the tile-roofed resort to take the half-mile-long driveway to the hotel. I always pull in for something cold to drink, and a rest. I'd suggest it to be the final stop but $200 to $300 a day is as steep as Dixville Notch Road. The guests here are usually three generations deep; whole families come for a week at a time. The surroundings and environment are something to relish. It is wonderful to stroll the grounds overlooking the lake and the Notch.

Inside L.L. Cote Hardware store in Errol, you'll find some fascinating taxidermy, not the least of which is an albino moose.

Late afternoon on the veranda (in season) can bring sumptuous hors d'oeuvres, like fresh strawberries and chocolate for dipping—no charge for guests, of course. The Balsams is a legend, which you can enjoy today.

When you hear the national election returns with reports that Dixville Notch has completed its voting ahead of the rest of the nation, this is where it has taken place. There's a special room in the hotel where the ballots are cast. It's worth a visit, as there are many interesting photos of political dignitaries.

Back out on Route 26, turn left to climb through Dixville Notch and ride the 12 miles to Errol. Just before town, check out Errol International Airport, with its tiny hangar. A solitary Cessna sat on the tarmac when I went by! The junction of Route 26 and Route 16 in Errol is a major crossroads for motor-cyclists and outdoor enthusiasts of all kinds. In these parts, there aren't many places to buy fuel and food, so just about everyone stops in Errol. In summer, the **Northern Exposure Restaurant** is jammed with motorcyclists and hik-ers. In winter, packs of snowmobiles take over the entire town. Don't pass up your chance to see the stuffed albino moose and other fascinating taxidermy in the **L.L. Cote Hardware** store on Main Street. Turn right heading south on Route 16 from Errol. Here the road follows every bend in the Androscoggin River, exposing pristine land, marsh, and riverbank. The only interruption is an occasional canoe or angler or moose in the river.

The 13 Mile Woods scenic area is a favorite with local bikers because of the turns, isolation, and remoteness. I chose to incorporate this run into the Northeast Loop. You are hardly disturbed traveling this thirty-mile stretch of road from Errol except by your own imagination . . . until you reach Berlin (pronounced BER-lin). Just north of Berlin, is the town of Milan (pronounced MY-lun). As you approach the town line between these two northern hamlets, look to a steep hill on your right. The 170-foot steel frame of the Nansen Ski Jump looms high above the horizon. It hasn't been used in ages, but more than forty years ago, stalwart ski jumpers soared high above the Androscoggin Valley on giant wooden skis!

Across the road from the jump is the **Nansen Wayside Park.** This 14-acre state park on the river is a great place to picnic, view the river, go fishing, or just relax. If you do stop at the park, be careful. The long gravel driveway can sometimes be a bit bumpy. Just in case you are ready to eat again, or maybe you'd like some ice cream, the **Northland Restaurant and**

Relax to the sounds of Beaver Brook Falls. It's open to the public, and a good place to set up a picnic.

Dixville notch not only forewarns but delivers!

Dairy Bar is just three miles south of the ski jump and park. This eatery is very popular with the locals. It features a huge menu including their famous haddock dinners (poached or fried), buffalo burgers, a wide sandwich selection, six different soups each day, homemade desserts, and great ice cream creations, to boot! In summer months you'll often see many motorcycles sporting Canadian license plates parked out front.

Berlin is dominated physically, economically, and socially by its paper mill. The physical presence is awesome, yet incongruous with the mountains in the background. I saw the paper mill from Mt. Washington, although at the time I didn't realize what it was; it dominated the valley even from that perspective. It's the only work in town. Stay upwind if you can! Paper is one of the largest polluting industries we have, and it smells it. Route 16 back to home base is a straight shot

➡ Side Trip to Mt. Washington

If you'd like to ride to the top of New England, the 16-mile round trip on the **Mt. Washington Auto Road** will set you back $8. (Passengers are extra.) I approached the toll booth with a mixture of apprehension and excitement. The ranger was just changing the weather board to up the wind gust velocity to 60 mph. I asked him what the story was. He said "Motorcycles are allowed up as long as the wind gusts stay below 65 mph."

It's only gusting to 60, averaging 35," said the ranger as I paid the toll, and received my THIS BIKE CLIMBED MT. WASHINGTON bike-sized bumper sticker. This was a good omen and confidence builder. The ranger thought I'd be successful!

The beginning of the route is simple enough: the road is paved, wooded on both sides, and immediately starts a steep climb. The signs on the descent side of the road before each pulloff state "cool brakes frequently." The degree of climb will make you understand why 4-wheeled vehicles need to make frequent stops on the descent. The steed felt comfortable in second gear until I broke the tree line.

The road alternates between roadbed and pavement from the tree line to the summit. The switchbacks and vistas caused me to alternate between first and second gears for the second four miles of the eight-mile climb. It's probably better to do your rubbernecking on the way down with the views and road in front of you. I had a car a few hundred yards ahead of me and wanted to keep that buffer, not only for safety reasons, but to make my ride steadier for not having to adjust to the pace of the car.

When I reached the summit, I pulled up next to five more steeds. They seemed to stake out a comfortable parking zone. Everywhere I turned was a photo opportunity, and this was just the parking lot!

Climb the stairs to "Tip Top Hill." The structure on it, the "Tip Top House," was a hotel in 1853 when you could only get to the summit by climbing. The hotel failed, though, and the Tip Top House became the publishing offices of the *Among The Clouds* newspaper until 1915. The carriage road was completed in 1861 and the Mt. Washington Cog Railroad was completed in 1869. The railroad's coal-fired steam engine still climbs its 37-percent grade—the second steepest in the world—on daily trips out of Bretton Woods. Most of the track is laid on wooden trestles.

The descent was all I anticipated. First gear the whole way down; I hardly had to apply the brakes. You'll genuinely appreciate the ability to do the same. The air is often heavy with the stinging odor of cooking car brakes. The view is unrivaled and the ride deliciously slow. I recommend the trip if the weather cooperates, which happens only a few precious days a year. ∎

Trip 11 Northeast Notches Loop

Distance *184 miles without side trips*

Highlights *River roads and scenic stops, an easy high country route*

The Route from White Lake State Park

0 mi From White Lake State Park, turn left onto Route 16 north

15.0 In Conway, turn left to stay on Route 16 north

26.0 In Glen, bear right to stay on Route 16 north

48.5 In Gorham, turn left to stay on Route 16 north

49.9 In Gorham, bear right to stay on Route 16 north

84.4 In Errol, turn right onto Route 26 east (If you want an alternate route, taking you through the Height-of-Land loop in the Rangeley Lake region of Maine, turn left onto Route 16 at mile 84.7. See alternate route description below.)

The good people at the Auto Road tollhouse will let you know if it's safe to ride to the top of the Northeast's tallest mountain and home of the "World's Worst Weather."

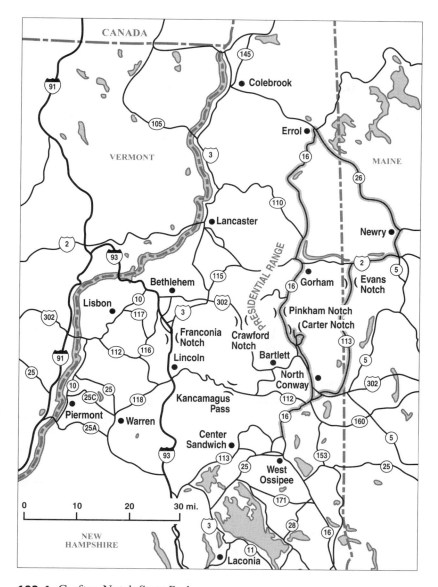

102.4 Grafton Notch State Park

114.9 At Newry, turn right onto Route 2 west (Height-of-Land alternate route rejoins here)

131.0 Just beyond Gilead, turn left onto Route 113 south

149.5 Turn left to stay on Route 113 south; Stowe Country Store is at intersection

160.0 Turn left to stay on Route 113 south into Fryeburg

161.3 In Fryeburg, turn left onto Route 302 south

169.1 In Conway, continue straight ahead onto Route 16 south

184.1 Arrive at White Lake State Park

Alternate Route via Height-of-Land and Rangeley Lake

0 mi At Errol, turn left onto Route 16 north at intersection of Routes 16 and 26

5.4 Lake Umbagog National Wildlife Refuge

35.8 Bear right onto Route 17 south toward Rumford

41.5 Turn left for a scenic view overlooking Rangeley Lake

47.1 Height of Land. Pull out on the right into the overlook of Lake Mooselookmeguntic

58.7 Coos Canyon

66.3 Swift River Falls on right—good picnic stop

71.5 Turn right onto Route 2 at Mexico

89.1 Rejoin main trip loop at Newry, Maine; continue on Route 2 west

This is a simple route that provides an easy outing with plenty of scenery. Route 16 is worthwhile from both directions. Going north this time, you travel upstream with better views of the Androscoggin River.

The day I rode north, I came upon three deer in the road. As I slowed, they broke for the woods. I decided to pull over and see if they would return if I was real still. While I was waiting, a bicyclist in full road gear came by heading south. I called to him about the deer. He pulled over for a chat.

The gentleman had silver hair and a well-tanned road-worn face. There was a uniqueness about him that was hard to place. I asked him where he was going, and he said "North Conway." I asked him where he was coming from and he smiled. It turned out he was returning from an eight-year circumnavigation of the world by bicycle. On this day he was going to make home. I was startled. I had to restrain myself from asking a million inane questions. Being on the road for only months at a time, I had to ask him what the toughest part of his travel was. He said it was struggling with the loneliness for the first five years. Bicycling is a solitary mode of transportation. I could relate but ever so slightly. In the end, he had his mission and I had mine, and off we went in separate directions, I a little less lonely for the camaraderie of aloneness.

The Rangeley Lake Scenic Overlook just before Height-of-Land offers a breathtaking view of the lakes and mountains in the northern wilderness.

At the intersection of Routes 16 and 26 at Errol, hang a right and go east into Maine. You will see a lot of Canadian license plates, for this is one of the routes to Old Orchard Beach from Montreal. Old Orchard Beach, in Maine, is a large Quebecois hangout.

If you prefer a longer ride, one with breathtaking views, follow the alternate Height-of-Land Loop, which diverges from our main trip at Errol.

Just after you enter the **Grafton Notch State Park,** you will find a number of waterfalls, swimming holes, and picnic areas throughout the park, so grab some grub back in Upton.

From Newry on Route 26 to Gilead on Route 2, the roadside gets more traveled and commercial. This stretch of commercialism is a small price to pay for getting to Route 113 south, a special road through **Evans Notch State Park.**

This is a narrow, smooth, and winding road that climbs to Evans Notch. The signs that warn you to watch out for logging trucks seem appropriate. Although I did not encounter any, I can't imagine one fitting on just their half of this asphalt alley. Without trucks and traffic, this road is a genuine find.

After Evans Notch, it's back to Conway and the short scoot home on Route 16.

(See Alternate Route via Height-of-Land and Rangeley Lake)

➡ Alternate Route via Height-of-Land and Rangeley Lake

If you have a little extra time and want to ride one of the prettiest ridge routes in western Maine, skip Grafton Notch and continue on Route 16 north by taking the sharp left at Errol. The road is serpentine and remote through soft pines, and skirts the Lake Umbagog (pronounced um-BAY-gog) National Wildlife Refuge, famous for its nesting eagles. You can rent kayaks for self-guided or guided tours of this pristine lake and for seeing the eagles.

After thirty-six miles of inspired riding, you will reach the town of Oquossoc and **The Gingerbread House Restaurant** on the left, a good place for a snack or lunch. Then, backtrack a block or two to pick up Route 17 south. The road climbs for a few miles to the ridge line where the vista suddenly opens up and takes your breath away. You'll want to stop at the spectacular overlooks to the Rangeley Lake valley on the left and Mooselookmeguntic Lake on the right at "Height-of-Land." As you descend off the ridge, you'll see Coos Canyon on the left, where you can actually pan for gold in the aptly named Swift River. Alternatively, join the local high diving competition from the straited rock platforms at the picnic area across from the Old Prospector's Mineral and Gift Shoppe. Another six miles and you'll spot the steam smokestacks from the mills at Mexico (Maine), and civilization.

The twin mill towns of Mexico and Rumford are not without interest. Turning right onto Route 2 west, you'll soon pass the Strathglass Park Historic District in Rumford with some fifty well-preserved brick homes, a planned community built in 1901 for the mill laborers of the Oxford Paper Company. Across the street, the Androscoggin River drops over a granite ledge to form dramatic Rumford Falls and provide the power to run the town's pulp and paper mills.

Route 2 west takes you to Newry, where you rejoin the original route, and proceed on toward charming Bethel, Maine.   ■

Places of Interest

Berlin

Northland Dairy Bar and Restaurant, Route 16. Phone 603-752-6210. Daily 11:00 a.m. to 8:00 p.m. Open year-round. A huge menu of good food and ice cream delights. Would you like fries with your bison burger? $

Colebrook

Shrine of Our Lady of Grace, Route 3. Phone 603-237-5511 for information on the blessing of the motorcycles. Motorcycle heaven, literally. There is no charge for visiting the Shrine. Donations are accepted.

Conway

Chinook Café, Route 16. Phone 603-447-6300. Open 8:00 a.m. to 3:00 p.m. Sunday-Tuesday, 8:00 a.m. to 9:00 p.m. Wednesday-Saturday Great homemade wraps and salads. Have a cozy dinner from their limited but unique menu. Sunday brunch is a worthy occasion. $$

Dixville Notch

The Balsams, Route 26. Phone 800-255-0600. Daily, year-round. A little bit of the Alps in America. Beautiful scenery, and luxury. A legend in its own time. $$$

On your way back through Conway, stop in to see Whitehorse Press, publishers of books and a catalog for motorcycling enthusiasts.

Errol

Northern Exposure Restaurant at the junction of Route 26 and Route 16. Phone 603-482-3468. Open year-round 5:00 a.m. to 8:00 p.m. Home cooking by the headwaters of the Androscoggin River. $$

Franconia

New England Ski Museum, Franconia Notch State Park. Phone 603-823-7177. Daily 9:00 a.m. to 5:00 p.m. Open May to October, and ski season if you put the spikes on the treads. If you are an enthusiast, videos and a history of how our species evolved from barrel slats. $$

Robert Frost Place, Ridge Road. Phone 603-823-8038. Daily 10:00 a.m. to 5:00 p.m. Open Memorial day to Columbus Day. Frost's farmhouse restored as a museum. $

Gorham

Loaf Around Bakery and Restaurant, 19 Exchange Street. Phone 603-466-2706. Perfect for a quick stop. $

Moose Brook State Park off Route 2, Jimtown Road. Phone 603-466-3860. Open mid-May to mid-October. Camping, swimming, hiking, fishing, and showers. $

Holderness

Squam Lake Natural Science Center, Route 113. Phone 603-968-7194. www.nhnature.org. Open daily from May through November 1st featuring four self-guided trails, native wildlife. Admission: adults $11; youth (3–15) $8; children under 3 are free.

Madison

Bill's Place Restaurant, Route 16. Phone 603-447-6747. Closed Monday. Open Tuesday through Saturday, 6:00 a.m. to 8:00 p.m., and Sunday 'til 3:00 p.m. Home of the $2.19 breakfast. Rider-friendly, home-style cooking. $

Milan

Nansen Wayside Park on Route 16. Phone 603-323-2087. Open daily year-round. Fourteen acres of Androscoggin River frontage for picnicking and fishing. No access fee.

North Conway

Horsefeathers Restaurant, "Center of the Known Universe." 603-356-6862. Open daily year-round. One of the most popular and longest-lasting venues for hearty food and drink, it has earned its place as a favored gathering spot in the Conway area.

Pinkham Notch

Mt. Washington Auto Road, Route 16. Phone 603-466-3988. 7:30 a.m. to 6:00 p.m. $8 per person. Weather permitting, it's a tale to tell!

Sanbornville

Poor People's Pub, Main Street. Phone 603-522-8378. Daily 11:00 a.m. to 10:00 p.m., opens Sunday at noon to 9:30. Year-round good pub grub. Always a couple of steeds outside. $$

Sugar Hill

Polly's Pancake Parlor, Route 117. Phone 603-823-5575. Daily 7:00 a.m. to 3:00 p.m., weekends till 7:00 p.m. Late April through late October. The best! $$$ (Good food but very pricey)

Sunset Hill House, Sunset Hill Road. Phone 603-823-5522. Daily year-round inn. For the view, get there before sunset! $$$

Tamworth

Rosie's Restaurant, Route 16. Phone 603-323-8611. Open daily for breakfast and lunch. Monday through Saturday 5:00 a.m. to 2:00 p.m., Friday nights from 4:00 p.m. to 8:00 p.m. Try the fish fry, it's exceptional! Open Sunday from 6:00 a.m. to 12:00 p.m. $

White Lake State Park, Route 16. Phone 603-323-7350. Late May through Columbus Day. First come, first served. On White Lake, swimming along with the other normal facilities. Well kept and centrally located. $12 per campsite.

Tilton

Tilt'n Diner, Route 3. Phone 603-286-2204. Open daily. Sunday through Thursday, 6:00 a.m. to 9:00 p.m., Friday and Saturday, 6:00 a.m. to 10:00 p.m. Home-style cooking, great specials, cheap prices. $

West Stewartstown

The Spa Restaurant & Outback Pub, Route 3. Phone 603-246-3039. Open year-round 3:00 a.m. (yes, that's a.m.!) to 9:00 p.m. Steaks and seafood with live entertainment. $$

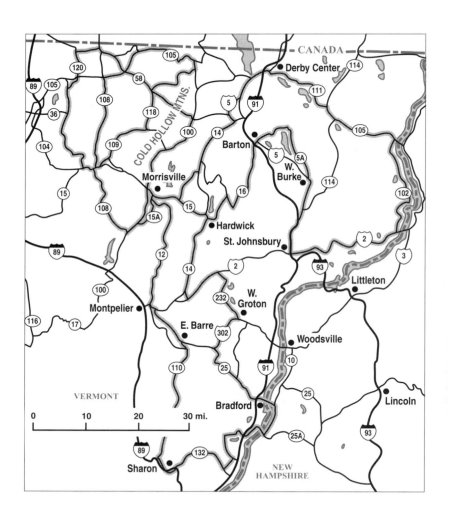

Twisting Northern Vermont

Vermont's four northern regions—the northern Green Mountains, the Northeast Kingdom, the Piedmont, and the Champlain Islands—differ widely from one another. In many ways you'll wonder if you're in the same state as you explore each of them on consecutive days. The northern Green Mountains and the Piedmont are known for their spectacular fall foliage, while the Northeast Kingdom allows you to get away from it all—don't expect any cell phone reception in "the Kingdom."

Morrisville, Hardwick, and St. Johnsbury are the gateways into what is known as the Northeast Kingdom. The Northeastern section of the state is considered the last bastion of true Vermont; both the terrain and local attitudes differ widely from those seen on other loops. This is a land of crystal-clear lakes and rural roads, where encountering traffic means going around the tractor. St. Johnsbury is filled with architectural gems and fine art, the legacy of the Fairbanks family. You ought to plan some time exploring the treasures on Main Street.

The northern portion of the Green Mountains holds some of the most enjoyable motorcycling roads in the state, including Route 108 through Smugglers Notch and the lesser-known Route 58 through Hazens Notch. Whether you are looking for twisty roads or beautiful scenery, the northern Green Mountains is the place to ride.

The Vermont Piedmont region is picture-postcard perfect with villages like Chelsea, Tunbridge, Strafford, and Thetford Hill. The roads, whether twisting through the maze of the central Piedmont or along the Connecticut River, are a delight. Montpelier, a state capitol whose population is less than most small New England villages, is an excellent place to stop and stretch your legs, get breakfast, or even ride to for supper and a movie.

I chose to make **Elmore State Park,** near Morrisville, Vermont, my base for this exploration. If you are looking for rural solitude, take the hiking trails up Mt. Elmore to the summit, where you'll be rewarded by stupendous views. By climbing the fire tower, you can nearly see forever. You can also rent canoes to explore Lake Elmore. If world-class gourmet dining strikes your interest, you'll want to ride to Stowe for the evening.

Trip 12 Northeast Kingdom Loop

Distance *206 miles without side trips*

Highlights *St. Johnsbury is an interesting stop on this loop, but mostly it's riding through extremely rural areas that range from cultivated land to the deep Northern Boreal Forest. The lakes, especially the ride along the shore of Lake Willoughby, are a special treat.*

The Route from Elmore State Park, Morrisville, Vermont

0.0 Turn left onto Route 12 north leaving Elmore State Park

3.6 Turn right onto Route 15A east (Park Street)

5.4 Turn right onto Route 15 east

17.5 At the stop light in Hardwick, turn left and go one short block on Route 15 east

17.6 Turn left onto Main Street, proceed over the railroad track, then to the police station and library

A farm shrouded in morning fog east of St. Johnsbury, Vermont.

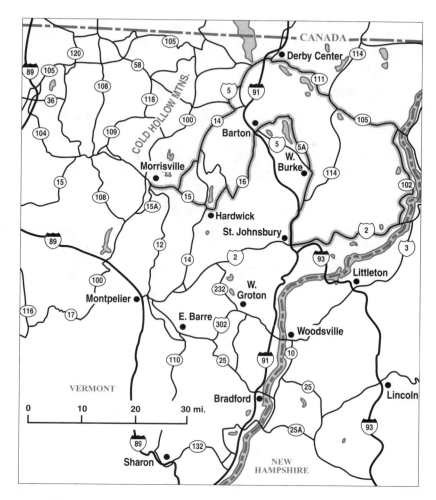

17.7 Turn right onto Church Street; as you proceed, it becomes Maple Street, then Center Road

24.0 In Greensboro, turn right around Willey's Store onto East Street

24.1 Turn right onto The Bend Road

26.8 At Greensboro Bend, turn left onto Route 16 north

42.4 At Barton, turn right onto Routes 16 north/5 south

42.6 Turn left and continue on Route 16 north

49.7 Near Westmore, turn right onto Route 5A south

60.1 At West Burke, bear left onto Route 5 south

76.9 In St. Johnsbury, turn left onto Concord Avenue

Riding north on Route 12 you're presented with a panoramic view of northern Vermont.

77.5   Turn left onto Route 2 east

103.6   Near Lancaster, proceed straight onto Route 102 north

126.3   At Bloomfield, turn left onto Route 105 west

142.3   At Island Pond, proceed straight onto Route 114 north

145.0   Where Route 111 joins Route 114, turn left onto Route 111 north

159.5   At Derby Center, turn right onto Routes 5A north/105 west

160.0   Turn left onto Routes 5 south/105 west

164.8   In Newport, turn left onto Third Street

164.9   Turn right onto Pleasant Street

165.7   Bear left onto Route 5 south

170.9   At Coventry, where Routes 5 and 14 split, bear right onto Route 14 south

188.5   Turn right onto Branch Road, which changes to North Wolcott Road, following signs to North Wolcott

197.0   Turn right onto Route 15 west

200.7   Turn left onto Route 15A east

202.5   Turn left onto Route 12 south

206.1   Turn right into Elmore State Park

The day begins with the beautiful vistas of the northern Green Mountain Range directly ahead and the expanse of the Northeast Kingdom stretching to the horizon on your left. Route 15A is a shortcut to Route 15 east, but if your fuel tank isn't topped off, you might want to take the loop through Morrisville on Route 100 and attend to it now. While you're at it, get some breakfast to fortify yourself for the long ride ahead.

Soon you'll reach poor Hardwick, often the butt of crude Vermont jokes, but we're not going to stop long enough to hear any of them. After making the left turn at the blinking red traffic light, the next left turn comes up as soon as you shift into second, and you're no more over the little bridge than you're making the right turn around the library.

Greensboro is situated on Lake Caspian and this beautiful gem of clear water is visible throughout the descent into the village. Laura H. Wild, Ann Stoddard, and Silas Mason were born here and there are more than a few famous names who reside here during the summers. **Willey's Store** is a rare establishment, the true general store where you can purchase car batteries, fishing equipment, groceries, appliances, and clothing. Make a right around Willey's Store and then a right by the post office to get to Route 16.

Looking south from North Beach on Lake Willoughby.

*Lake Memphremagog was an active smuggling route during prohibition. The city of
Newport is the southern port on this lake, which stretches north into Quebec.*

About six miles north on Route 16, and just past Horse Pond, there is an
expanse of cattails and a granite historic site marker. This used to be the site
of Long Pond, but in 1810 a group of local residents decided to direct the
outflow of water to run into the Barton River to help power the local mill.
The trench for the new stream had been dug, but when the men tried to
breech the bank of the pond they hit quicksand and Long Pond began to
move. In fifteen minutes, two square miles of water rushed north with a
sixty-foot-high wave front racing through the towns of Glover and Barton
and continuing all the way to Lake Memphremagog. The surface water has
never returned and this expanse of cattails and quicksand is now known as
Runaway Pond.

Glover is best known for Peter Schumann's radical religious-political
Bread and Puppet Theater. The theater troupe moved here in 1974 and a
museum has now been established in a converted barn where their giant
neo-medieval puppets are on display.

In Barton, Route 16 north makes a hard right turn and briefly combines
with Route 5 south before breaking away crossing the railroad tracks and
climbing the hill. Crystal Lake can be seen to the left.

Mt. Pisgah and Lake Willoughby seen from the South Beach along Route 5A.

Coming down to the north end of Lake Willoughby is an experience and you might wish to pull into the parking lot for North Beach to appreciate its beauty. Like the Finger Lakes of New York, Lake Willoughby and Crystal Lake were carved by the advancing mile-and-a-half wall of glacial ice during the last Ice Age, but only here is the cutting of the scarp plainly visible. It's also a deep and cold body of water where lake trout grow to trophy size. Stop into any of the small convenience stores along Route 5A and you'll see photos posted on the bulletin boards that define the fish that didn't get away.

Route 5A goes south along the very edge of the lake; in places it's even cut into the very sides of Mt. Pisgah. It's such a scenic stretch of highway that you'll probably want to stop three or four times just to take pictures; with each turn of the road the vista seems to get more breathtaking.

The run down Route 5 will naturally feel anticlimactic after this, especially as traffic thickens close to St. Johnsbury. The quickest way through this city is to take a left at the second traffic light, cross over the Passumpsic River on Concord Street, and then continue east on Route 2. There are even picnic tables along the river in Fred Mold Memorial Park for a delightful break.

In 1830 Thaddeus Fairbanks invented the platform scale to weigh hemp (in those days it was used to make rope) and the Fairbanks family became very wealthy. Part of their legacy was the establishment of the (Franklin) **Fairbanks Museum,** one of the finest classic natural history museums still in existence. The public library, the **Athenaeum,** was built as a present to the city from Horace Fairbanks; the oldest unaltered art gallery in the United States is attached to it. *The Domes of Yosemite* by Albert Bierstadt, *The Views from South Mountain in The Catskills* by Sanford Gifford, and works by Thomas Waterman Wood and Asher Durand are some of the great pieces of American art to be discovered there. A rare E. Howard Street clock, which was once located in Grand Central Station, a Civil War memorial designed by Larkin Mead, stained-glass windows in the South Methodist Church by Lewis Comfort Tiffany, classic Victorian homes built by noted architect Lambert Packard, and much more are to be found along Main Street. The easiest way to reach Main Street is to bear right at the first traffic light and climb Hastings Hill or to take a right turn at the second set of lights and go up Sand Hill. At the southern end of Main Street, Eastern Avenue (Route 2 east) goes down the hill, through the downtown area, and past Concord Avenue. On the way out of the city you'll notice **Maple Grove Farms of Vermont,** the oldest and largest maple sugar candy factory in the world, and a place to learn about Vermont's maple sugar industry.

The next 26 miles is a fast run to the Connecticut River. Route 2 is the main thoroughfare from Vermont to Bangor, Maine, and the traffic can be heavy at times. Continue straight, following the river north on Route 102. You'll encounter very little traffic on this road and you can have a great time on the sweepers or just enjoying the scenery. As soon as you turn onto Route 105 and leave the river, you're into the Northern Boreal Forest, a land of conifers, bogs, almost no people, and lots and lots of moose (or is it meese?). These lands are owned by various paper companies who manage and log hundreds of square miles of forest land.

The village of Island Pond is named after the lake on the edge of town and its 11-acre wooded island. There's a public beach and picnic tables with barbecue pits should you choose to take a break. This was once the headquarters of the Grand Trunk Railway, but the exquisite stone depot and vast rail yards are all that remain of that famous line.

Route 114 goes north into the remote woods, but turning onto Route 111 leads you around the gorgeous Seymour Lake and some of the prettiest country in the Northeast Kingdom. Touring this deserted, winding road with gorgeous views will make your day.

Newport, once a famous port on the south end of Lake Memphremagog, is the commercial hub of the region. Riding through the bustling downtown is like going back in time to the early 1960s. This is a downtown of owner-operated businesses and not the series of chain stores that have so frequently taken over small town commercial centers. The signs for Route 5 south are clearly posted as you ride through a residential section, but almost before you know it you're back on open highway.

Route 14 briefly merges with Route 5 in Coventry. Bear right to continue south on Route 14 along the edge of the Lowell Mountains. Slightly less than two miles south of North Craftsbury Road, turn right. This road is one known only to locals, but like most of these small town roads, it's officially known as Branch Road when heading south and North Wolcott Road when going north. In local conversations it is simply called Wolcott Road. It's an enjoyable ride as the pavement follows the Wild Branch River. Finally it runs between two silos in a farmer's backyard and junctions at Route 15.

Route 15 east to Route 15A and Route 12 retrace the first few miles taken this morning, but riding in the opposite direction provides very different scenic views. Once again, the choice is yours whether to ride into Morrisville and enjoy supper or to head directly back to the campsite and cook your own.

Route 111 skirts beautiful Lake Seymour in Morgan.

Trip 13   Northern Green Mountains Loop

Distance *213 miles with options to shorten the distance*

Highlights *More twisty roads than most riders ever dream of, coupled with two of the most beautiful notch roads in the state are the main features of this ride. It also offers scenic vistas and leisurely touring at its best. This particular loop also has a couple of options that can shorten its overall distance—but why would you?*

A scenic view looking northeast toward Canada from Route 242.

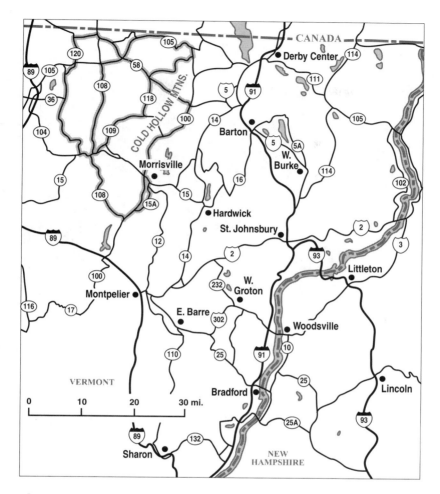

The Route from Elmore State Park, Morrisville, Vermont

0.0 Turn left onto Route 12 north when leaving Elmore State Park

2.6 Turn left onto Mt. Elmore Road and immediately turn right onto Washington Highway (Street)

4.2 In Morrisville, turn left onto Randolph Street

7.1 Continue straight across Childress Village Road

7.8 At intersection, turn right onto Randolph Road

10.6 Proceed to Route 100 south

13.6 At Stowe, turn right onto Route 108 north (Mountain Road)

Long Pond is located near the junction of Route 109 at Route 118.

30.8 At Jeffersonville, bear right at the traffic island onto Main Street to stay on Route 108 north

31.1 Proceed across Route 15. Stay on Route 108 north

31.5 Turn right onto Route 109 north

46.5 Turn right onto Route 118 south

53.1 At Eden, turn left onto Route 100 north

62.4 At Lowell, turn left onto Route 58 west

72.8 Turn right and then, across the bridge, immediately turn right again onto Route 242 east

84.4 At Jay, turn left onto Cross Road

85.9 Bear left onto Route 105 west

104.7 Bear right onto Berkshire Center Road (Route 118 north)

111.4 Proceed straight on Route 108 north

112.1 At East Franklin, turn left onto Route 120 west

112.7 Turn left to continue on Route 120 west

112.9 Where Routes 120 and 236 split, bear right to stay on Route 120 west

122.6 Proceed straight across Route 105 onto North Sheldon Road

123.6 Turn right onto Sheldon Road

126.1 Turn left onto Main Street; it becomes North Road

131.7 At Fairfield, proceed across Route 36 onto South Road; it becomes Fairfield Road, then becomes Cambridge Road, and then becomes Pumpkin Harbor Road

145.8 Near Cambridge, turn left onto Route 15 east

148.3 Turn left onto Route 108 north

167.5 At Enosburg Falls, turn right onto Route 105 east

173.6 At East Berkshire, turn right onto Route 118 south; the road passes through Montgomery Center and Belvedere Corners; stay on Route 118 south

195.6 At Eden, turn right onto Route 100 south

204.9 At Hyde Park, turn left onto Routes 100 south/15 east

208.0 Turn right to stay on Route 100 south

209.2 In Morrisville, turn left onto Route 12 south

212.9 Turn right into Elmore State Park

This round barn on Route 12 in Elmore is one of only a handful surviving in Vermont. Vermont's unique nineteenth-century barns are rapidly disappearing from the landscape.

'e begins by heading north and around the end of Mt. Elmore to ᴜtowe by the back roads. Route 100 quickly brings you into the center of Stowe village and then up the Mountain Road where all the services one could expect of a town that advertises itself as the "Ski Capitol of the East" are to be found. Some of the best gourmet and specialty restaurants in Vermont will be found on Route 108 between the center of town and the ski slopes.

The riding fun begins once you pass the ski area and enter the Mt. Mansfield State Forest and begin to climb into **Smugglers Notch,** so named from the popular trail used to smuggle goods and livestock to Canada in defiance of Thomas Jefferson's Embargo Act of 1807. The road snakes around massive boulders that have fallen from the cliffs above and no matter how good a rider you might be, when you exit that last severely banked curve and reach the top of the Notch, you want to be in first or second gear and going about 10 mph. Pedestrians, hikers, and drivers rubbernecking at climbers scaling the cliffs, combined with blind corners flanked by solid rock and the narrowest paved highway in the state, make this a place to ride defensively.

As you begin your descent on a hot summer day, slow down and stay to the right side of the road to catch a cold shower from the waterfall as you pass; conversely, on a freezing autumn morning stay close to the center lane to avoid black ice. The rest of the way to Jeffersonville is an easy and quick descent.

A view of Smugglers Notch from the Mt. Mansfield Toll Road shows the northern end of the Green Mountain Range.

Large boulders form part of the scenic landscape in Smugglers Notch and the road is forced to weave around and between them.

Route 109 is one of those highways the local riders try to keep secret. It's almost all curves and corners and if you don't get stuck behind a school bus or farm tractor it can be an exciting stretch of road. When you reach Route 118 you have two options: the most scenic is a 26-mile loop of which about ten are gravel road; the other option is a quick 8-mile run on Route 118 north to Montgomery Center. If you're riding as a group this option allows anyone who doesn't wish to tackle the gravel road through Hazens Notch to wait for the rest over a cup of coffee and breakfast in Montgomery Center.

For the bold souls, it's a quick, scenic, and rather fun trip down Route 118 south to Route 100 north, then to the turn onto Route 58 west by the little green gazebo in the village of Lowell. Not as stupendous as Smugglers Notch and not as challenging a ride as the Appalachian Gap, Hazens Notch is the most northern, and perhaps the most scenic, road through the Green Mountains. Besides, if you're going to boast about riding Vermont's famous gaps you don't want to answer no to the question, "Oh yeah, have you ridden over Hazens Notch?"

Now back down to Route 118 in Montgomery Center and at the southern end of Route 242 you're about to be let into another secret. The following—Routes 242 east, 105 west, and 118 south—form a loop around Jay Peak where Vermont and Quebec riders test their new Hayabusas, Ducatis, and Bahn-burners. This route offers some incredible views into Canada, but I suggest you either slow down and sightsee or keep your eyes to the pavement and boogie. What an exciting run it is down the backside of Jay to Stevens Mill without a single house, driveway, or joining road to consider!

Cliffs and curves make Route 108 through Smugglers Notch one of the most popular motorcycle roads in Vermont.

Instead of taking Route 118 south, bear left onto Berkshire Center Road (Route 118 north) and enjoy the narrow roads that interconnect these tiny rural villages. This agricultural area is just a couple miles from Canada; farm roads cross the border like it doesn't officially exist. After rounding the northern end of Lake Carmi, it's time to head south through the rolling countryside that lies between the Champlain Valley and the western edge of the Green Mountains.

The tiny village of Sheldon has the distinction of being part of the northernmost action of the Civil War. On October 19, 1864, a small group of 22 Confederate soldiers lead by Bennett Young infiltrated St. Albans, robbed the bank of over $200,000, shot and killed a local bystander, and torched the covered bridge in Sheldon to cover their retreat. They escaped to Canada where they found official sanctuary.

The section of this tour from Fairfield to Cambridge on narrow, twisting town roads with almost no traffic offers the kind of touring I like best. This ends when reaching Route 15 in Cambridge. The modern bridge over the Lamoille River replaced the magnificent covered bridge that now graces the entrance to the Shelburne Museum on Route 7. But head east because **Jana's Cupboard** is only a couple of miles away.

After picking up something to eat at Jana's Cupboard deli—and some pastries for a midnight snack—head west to the intersection of Routes 15 and 108. Those who feel that they've done enough riding for today can either head back through Smugglers Notch on Route 108 east or continue on Route 15 west to Morrisville (15.6 miles). But . . . if you want to add a few more choice miles to your day, head north on Route 108. From Jeffersonville to Enosburg Falls is one of the best routes for viewing fall foliage in the northern part of the state. There are only a handful of round barns that have survived and you pass two of them: one on Route 108 and one on Route 12. Old-timers tell you that they were built round so that the devil couldn't corner ya, but actually they were part of the great agricultural experimentation that occurred at the end of the nineteenth century. The circular shape was meant to be more efficient for milking and feeding the cows, but this design proved to be far more costly and much more difficult to heat than conventional rectangular barns.

Route 15 east brings you to Route 118, where riding south will let you experience the last of the Jay Peak loop. Retracing your path to Route 100, turn right and continue south to Morrisville. The **Charlmont Restaurant** is a good place for supper before logging the last five miles home to Elmore State Park.

Route 58 through Hazens Notch is the least traveled Green Mountain Gap road.

Trip 14 Vermont Piedmont Loop

Distance *193 miles*

Highlights *The smallest state capitol in the United States and the granite quarries that make Barre the "Granite Capitol of the World" are just two of the sites to be visited on this loop. Mostly, prepare for wonderful touring roads and picture-postcard views.*

The Route from Elmore State Park, Morrisville, Vermont

0.0 Turn right onto Route 12 south leaving Elmore State Park

21.8 In Montpelier, turn left onto Spring Street

21.9 Bear right at the round-about onto Main Street

22.5 Turn left onto Routes 302 east/2 east

24.3 Bear right and continue on Route 302 east

29.1 Bear left onto Washington Street (Route 302 east)

The White River alongside Route 14 is a multi-use recreational river and a very popular one for trout fishing and tubing.

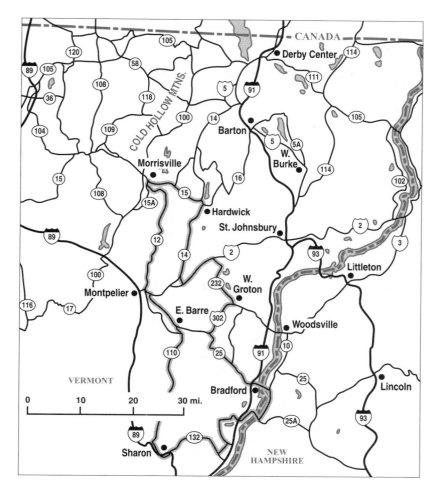

32.9 In East Barre, turn right onto Route 110S and immediately bear left

59.8 Turn left onto Route 14 south

64.7 In Sharon, turn left onto Route 132 east

80.1 Turn left onto Academy Road

83.3 At Thetford Center, turn left onto Route 113 west

88.6 At Post Mills, turn right onto Route 244 east

94.4 Turn left onto Route 5 north

103.0 Near Bradford, turn left onto Route 25 west

120.3 Turn right onto Route 302 east

135.4 About a mile past West Groton, turn left onto Route 232 north

148.8 Turn left onto Route 2 west

157.3 At Plainfield, bear right onto Route 214 north

159.3 At North Montpelier, turn right onto Route 14 north

175.4 In Hardwick, turn left and continue on Routes 14 north/15 west

176.5 Proceed on Route 15 west

187.5 Near Morrisville, turn left onto Route 15A west

189.3 In Morrisville, turn left onto Route 12 south

192.9 Turn right into Elmore State Park

The first 22 miles on Route 12 follow the North Branch of the Winooski River to Montpelier. This is moose country and the earlier you leave in the morning the more likely you are to see one of these giant creatures alongside this stretch of road. The mountains to the right are the Worcester Range; Stowe Valley is on their western side.

You can either turn left and bear right to continue through Montpelier on Main Street, or stay straight on Elm Street until reaching State Street. If you stay on Elm Street, the Vermont Capitol building is just up State Street to your right and Main Street is the next block to your left. This is the smallest state capitol in the United States and the population has overtones of a late '60s hippy refuge. This is also home to the New England Culinary Institute (NECI), just one of many businesses that were founded by former Goddard College students, teachers, and administrators. At the traffic light (the only one in downtown) **La Brioche,** NECI's café for training students is on one corner, while the **Coffee Corner** occupies another. For a continental-style breakfast try La Brioche, but for the hungry-man special, the Coffee Corner is a must.

(See Side Trip to the Granite Quarries)

The first 5.8 miles of Route 110 are not at all exciting, but once you crest the height-of-the-land in Washington, it becomes a premier motorcycle-touring highway as it winds down this high valley in the heart of Vermont's Piedmont Range.

Route 14 follows the White River south from Royalton to Sharon. There are a number of pulloffs along the highway and the sculpted rocks, deep pools, and fast-moving water are almost irresistible on a hot summer day. You'll probably see people fly fishing, tubing, and canoeing as you ride along the riverbank. Just a mile south of the junction of Route 110 is a left turn leading up the hill to the birthplace of the Mormon prophet, Joseph Smith.

The E.L. Smith Quarry in Graniteville is part of the Rock of Ages tour. This is the largest (50-acres) and deepest active granite quarry in the world.

➡ Side Trip to the Granite Quarries

Continue straight through the traffic lights by the hospital onto Airport Road. At the end of Airport Road (3.4 miles), turn right onto Miller Road and continue for 1.5 miles to Route 63. Turn left and proceed down the hill. Directly ahead is the Rock of Ages quarry on Quarry Hill. Once you reach the bottom of the hill, cross Route 14 and climb Middle Road. At the stop sign on top of the hill, the finishing sheds and quarry are on your left. Seven-tenths of a mile farther is the **Rock of Ages Visitors Center** and parking lot. To reach Route 110, backtrack 0.2 mile, turn right onto Donahue Road and follow the signs to Route 110. Turn right onto Route 110 in East Barre. ∎

The courthouse in Chelsea on Route 110 is still the county seat, which make this village a "Cheshire town."

In Sharon, a left turn onto Route 132 takes you under the I-89 highway and then on a fantastic climb up one side of the mountain and a very steep (14 percent grade) descent to South Strafford. Route 132 continues winding through the maze of the Piedmont before making a long descent past the Union Village Flood Control Dam. Turn left onto Academy Road through the Union Village Covered Bridge, which forms the middle of an S-curve, and past the Thetford Academy (established 1819) and into Thetford Hill. This is a classic Vermont village. This was the home of the famous philanthropist George Peabody and that of Henry Wells who founded Wells Fargo in this small hill village.

The ride around the north shore of Lake Fairlee along Route 244 is another enjoyable stretch of road. Route 5 also has its high points, especially those looking over the Connecticut River with panoramic views into New Hampshire and the narrow passage squeezed between the cliffs of Sawyer Mountain and the river. Lake Morey lies just behind the great cliffs of the Palisades in the village of Fairlee. Captain Samuel Morey invented both the rotary steam engine (1793) and the internal combustion engine (1835). He was the first person to successfully build a steamship and Robert Fulton's Clermont (the second steamship to carry passengers on an established route, not the first) was built from Morey's designs. Rumor has it that Samuel Morey sank the very first steamship in his namesake lake.

From Bradford to Groton, it's just over thirty miles of very enjoyable touring with the last mile or so along the South Branch of the Wells River having deceptively tight corners. Be prepared to scrape both pegs on this section of road.

Route 232 north through the Groton State Forest is another Vermont road you'll not soon forget. This road is fun on any bike at any speed but one that commands respect and a degree of skill if pushing past the posted speed limit. Corners arrive unexpectedly and often in conjunction with frost heaves or slight rises in the road, either of which can get you airborne while the pavement changes direction.

The eight miles on Route 2 west allow you to catch your breath, except for a couple of unexpected tight corners on Route 214. In Plainfield, Route 214 goes past Goddard College, the experimental college that influenced mainstream universities throughout the United States. A shadow of its former self, the reality of Goddard College in its heyday was far stranger than fiction.

Route 14 follows the eastern edge of the Woodbury Mountains and is the northwestern demarcation line for the Vermont Piedmont. In any other New England state, this section of Route 14 would be considered a choice motorcycle touring road, but you already know better.

At the blinking red traffic light in Hardwick, turn left following Route 15 west to Morrisville, then Route 12 back to the campsite. If you still have energy remaining after today's tour, consider hiking one of the many trails leading to the summit of Mt. Elmore to watch the sunset or renting a canoe and spending the evening exploring the shore of Lake Elmore. As much fun as these Vermont roads are to ride, some of most scenic places in Vermont still require either a paddle or "shank's mare" to explore.

A beautiful vintage barn in Tunbridge adds to the charm of the ride on Route 110.

Places of Interest

Barre

Rock of Ages Visitor's Center, 773 Graniteville Road, Graniteville.
Phone 802-476-3119. Open May 1 through October 31, Monday–Saturday 8:30 a.m.–5:00 p.m. www.rockofages.com. Although a new museum is being created in the old Jones & Lamson stone sheds on the
northern edge of the city, the story of Barre's granite industry is best
experienced on the edge of this largest and deepest granite quarry in the
world. Tours are offered of a working quarry and the famous Rock of
Ages stone sheds where master carvers create some of the finest
memorials in the world.

Elmore

Elmore State Park, open mid-May to October 15. $15–$22 night.
45 tent sites and 15 lean-tos. Phone 802-888-2982. This is one of Vermont's most beautiful state parks and offers the rural pleasures of either
canoeing on Elmore Lake or hiking to the top of Mt. Elmore to enjoy
spectacular views of the Green Mountains.

Greensboro

Willey's Store. Phone 802-533-2621. Open Monday–Friday 7:00
a.m.–5:30 p.m., Saturday and Sunday 8:00 a.m.–5:30 p.m.. This is a
real general store, not a touristy re-creation. If you've never experienced shopping in such an establishment, you should consider spending
a few minutes exploring this anachronism.

Jeffersonville

Jana's Cupboard Delicatessen and Bakery. Also, Jana's Restaurant (next door), Route 15. Phone 802-644-5454. The best deli and bakery in the area and well worth the stop. There are plenty of beautiful
places to enjoy a picnic, so a stop at Jana's is almost essential when
touring northern Vermont.

Montpelier

Coffee Corner, 83 Main Street. Phone 802-229-9060.
La Brioche Bakery & Café, 89 Main Street. Phone 802-229-0443.
Both are great places to have breakfast and get a sense of the eclectic
mix of residents who live and work in the smallest state capitol in the

United States. The Coffee Corner is owned and managed by graduates of the New England Culinary Institute, while La Brioche is part of the school and you can watch students preparing delicious pastries in the kitchen from the vantage of a picture window.

Morrisville

The Charlmont Resturant, Route 15. Phone 802-888-4242. A family restaurant that has been a Morrisville landmark for many decades. Conveniently located just a few minutes north of the campsite, it is the perfect place to end a day of touring.

St. Johnsbury

Fairbanks Museum, Main Street. Phone 802-748-2372. www.fairbanksmuseum.org. This is one of the finest small natural history museums in the country and harkens back to an earlier time when this type of museum brought the world closer to residents of remote places like St. Johnsbury.

St. Johnsbury Athenaeum, Main Street. Phone 802-748-8291. A great rarity; entering this public library is like stepping back in time. It also has the oldest unaltered gallery in the United States. An entire book could be written about this one location.

Maple Grove Farms of Vermont, 1006 Portland Street (Route 2) open 7 days a week, daily tours Monday–Friday Phone 802-748-5141. www.maplegrove.com. This is where commercial marketing of maple sugar candy began and remains the largest producer of maple sugar candy in the world. If you have a sweet tooth, yum!

Anthony's Diner, 321 Railroad Street (across the street from the old railroad station). Phone 802-748-3613. Open for breakfast, lunch and dinner, this little gem is head and shoulders above the norm. Breakfast specialties include skillet fried dishes and biscuits that will start your day off right. Save room at lunch for home-baked pies that will melt in your mouth. A trip to Anthony's alone makes the trip to St. Johnsbury worthwhile, but there's so much more to see here.

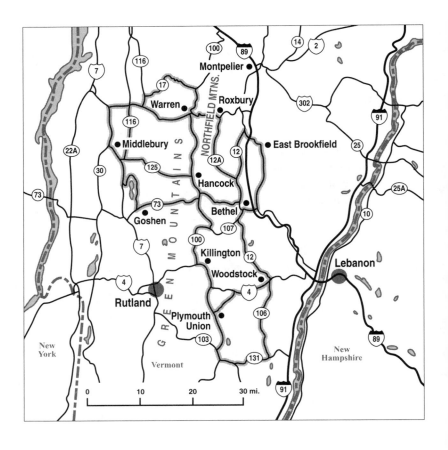

Closing Green Mountain Gaps

The Green Mountain Gaps are a natural extension of either the Lakes Journey, the Berkshires Journey, or the Northern Vermont Journey. Southeast of Lake Champlain, and due north of the Berkshires, the two loops of this journey crisscross the Green Mountain National Forest. **The Long Trail,** a 270-mile primitive footpath that inspired the Appalachian Trail, follows the central ridge of the Green Mountains and bisects our loops. The southern portion of the Long Trail, coinciding with the Appalachian Trail in the Berkshires, is the oldest long-distance footpath in the United States and contains some of the steepest, most rugged climbs in the Northeast.

Where the other journeys may be thought of as marathons, this mountain climb from valley to mountain crest journey is a wind sprint. In a relatively compact space of 350 miles, if you consolidate the two loops (shall we call it a loop-de-loop), you will tame five gaps, twice. The fun of crossing these gaps twice is the distinctly different terrain on each side of the mountain.

For example, going west across the Lincoln Gap, the east side is a two-mile ascent complete with sharp turns, hairpins, and ridge views on your right near the crest. Crossing the gap, the descent on the west side is very steep, very short, and straight through a stand of pine with a dirt roadbed to greet you at the bottom.

Going east, the west side of Lincoln Gap is the steepest climb I rode in Vermont, while the east side provides a long second-gear descent and valley view. Two entirely different challenges. All the gaps are like this, with one side being sharp and steep and the other a long, luxurious climb.

Since you'll be passing many of the highlighted places of interest more than once, you may not always reach them at an appropriate time to stop. For example, you will pass **Texas Falls,** a small, remote picnic area and trail on Route 125, in the early morning on the Southern Gap Loop and in the afternoon on the Northern Gap Loop. The first time you pass a place of interest, I will highlight it; however, I will remind you at the more appropriate time on either loop.

Home base for this journey is **Branbury State Park** at the east end of 1,035-acre Lake Dunmore in Brandon, Vermont. In addition to 42 campsites, the park has a large beach for that early morning or late evening dip after a hard day's ride. In early fall, you will probably be the only one there.

Trip 15 Southern Gap Loop

Distance *162 miles*

Highlights *A variety of road types ranging from narrow twisting pavement to scenic valley highways along rivers. Calvin Coolidge's birthplace, the village of Woodstock, and the floating bridge in Brookfield are special sites along the way.*

The Route from Branbury State Park

0.0 Turn right onto Route 53 north out of Branbury State Park

3.9 Turn right onto Route 7 north

6.7 At Middlebury, turn right onto Route 116 north

7.2 Turn right onto Route 125 east

22.6 At Hancock, turn right onto Route 100 south

46.4 At Killington, bear left onto Routes 100 south/4 east

52.6 At West Bridgewater, turn right and proceed on Route 100 south

57.9 At Plymouth Union, turn left onto Route 100A north

Route 125 through the Green Mountain National Forest is also known as the Robert Frost Highway.

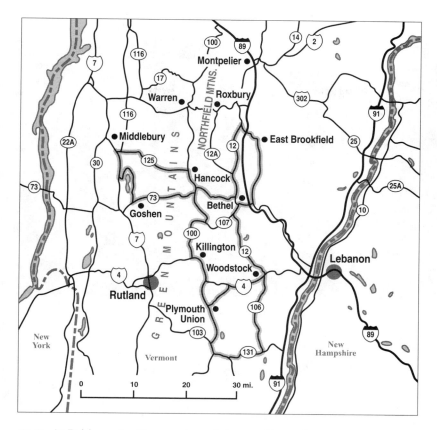

64.8 At Bridgewater Corners, turn right onto Route 4 east

72.9 At Woodstock, turn left onto Elm Street, which becomes Route 12 north

89.3 Near Bethel, turn right onto Routes 12 north/107 east

91.1 At Bethel, turn right and proceed on Route 107 east

94.5 At North Royalton, turn left onto Route 14 north

110.0 At East Brookfield, turn left onto Route 65 west

115.1 At the junction, turn left onto Route 12 south

130.7 Beyond Beanville, turn right onto Camp Brook Road

141.1 At Rochester, turn left onto Route 100 south

142.3 Turn right onto Route 73 west

155.8 Beyond Goshen, turn right onto Route 53 north

161.6 Turn right into Branbury State Park

Stop and enjoy a walk along the Robert Frost Interpretive Trail.

Route 53, with its narrow pavement and overhanging tree branches providing cool relief on a hot summer day, is a small lake road typical of access roads to summer cottages everywhere and a marked contrast to the busy Route 7 it leads to. From East Middlebury, Route 125 makes a rapid three-mile climb up the western side of the Green Mountains along Middlebury Gorge to Ripton, then a more leisurely climb for the next 5.5 miles to the crest of the Middlebury Gap at 2,149 feet above sea level.

This section of Route 125 is also known as the **Robert Frost Memorial Highway.** In 1920 Robert Frost helped found the Breadloaf School of English at Middlebury College. Two decades later he purchased a small farm with a cabin in Ripton as his summer retreat. Barely two miles beyond Ripton is a turn into a small parking lot for the Robert Frost Interpretive Trail, a one-mile walking trail with the wilderness scenes that inspired Frost and the corresponding poems—a place to ponder or impress your friends with your new literary prowess ("And miles to go before I sleep, and miles to go before I sleep"). Just beyond, in a turnout with picnic tables under the pine trees, a state historic sign notes that the poet laureate's cabin was located nearby. A quarter of a mile farther is a much more impressive tribute: the yellow clapboard buildings of **Middlebury College's Breadloaf campus** where the prestigious Breadloaf Writer's Conference takes places every summer.

After cresting the gap, the highway makes a quick, but gentle descent. The turn for Texas Falls is clearly marked on the north side of Route 125. It's only a half-mile up a narrow paved road and is a great place to stretch your legs, have a picnic, or just relax.

The **Old Hancock Hotel** building at the corner of Route 125 and Route 100 contains the Vermont Home Bakery and is a preferred local eating spot and rider rendezvous. Check out the tiny bookstore while waiting for your meal. I got sandwiches to go and ran up to Texas Falls.

Route 100, which runs from just north of the Vermont/Massachusetts border to just a few miles south of Newport, is a popular motorcycle touring highway. This section from Hancock to Plymouth Union offers some long straight sections along valley floors and twisting climbs to elevation, especially the stretch from Pittsburg to Killington (Route 4).

Texas Falls is a beautiful retreat from the cares of the everyday world. Pick up a sandwich from the Vermont Home Bakery and ride to Texas Falls for a picnic.

The village of Plymouth is the birthplace of President Calvin Coolidge. The small house with the weathered clapboards was where he was born and spent the first years of his life, while the "Summer White House" was located above the general store to which the house is attached.

Federal-style brick buildings face the oval green in downtown Woodstock.

The Floating Bridge at East Brookfield is a unique riding experience. Don't worry about the rain gear; this water flows up.

Route 100A runs from Plymouth Union through Plymouth Notch to West Bridgewater. This area was the site of Vermont's famous gold rush of 1856 and placer gold is still found in the streams of this township. The village of Plymouth is the home of Calvin Coolidge, the 30th President of the United States. Calvin Coolidge ascended to the presidency upon the death of President Warren G. Harding. He was vacationing at the family home in Plymouth when a messenger arrived from nearby Bridgewater (there were no phones or electricity in Plymouth at that time) with the news. In the early hours of August 3, 1923, by kerosene lamplight in the parlor of the home he grew up in, Calvin Coolidge was sworn in without fanfare as president of the United States by his father, John Coolidge, a notary public.

Pick up Route 4 in West Bridgewater by the general store and follow the Ottauquechee River to the village of Woodstock. Beautiful Federal-style buildings, art galleries, and unique stores abound here. This is a very upscale community, which is still dominated by Rockefeller interest.

Route 14 twists through Williamstown Gulf, an enjoyable alternative route for those not wishing to risk the crossing of the Floating Bridge on Sunset Lake in Brookfield.

At the end of Elm Street, you pick up Route 12 north. On the north side of the black iron bridge is the Rockefeller estate, and around the corner is **Billings Farm,** one of the best preserved experimental farms of the late nineteenth century.

Now it's a fast run to Bethel. Route 107 follows the White River and leads through the village of Bethel, under Interstate 89, and junctions at Route 14 by Eaton's Sugar House. Route 14 is a road favored by local motorcyclists, but one that visitors to the state are rarely aware of. There's a picnic table next to the covered bridge, just 5.5 miles from the junction of Route 107, and it's another great place to take a break and have a picnic lunch.

The general store at Bridgewater Corners is a great place to stop and pick up a snack, a cup of coffee, or long conversation.

Route 65 climbs Bear Mountain from East Brookfield. The pavement turns to gravel as you enter into the tiny village of Brookfield and come to the famous **Floating Bridge,** a wooden poontoon bridge that crosses Sunset Lake by literally floating on its surface. CAUTION: stay on the wooden tire tracks, which are usually submerged on either end of the bridge. This wood can be slippery with green algae and usually there are people fishing from it.

On the north side of the east end of the bridge is Hippopotamus Park. There resides a small white granite sculpture of two hippos, entitled Father & Son, created by Jim Sardonis. This white granite looks similar to marble and is quarried in Bethel.

Route 65 west of the Floating Bridge turns to dirt roadbed for about 2.5 miles, just after cresting the west side of Sunset Lake. This gravel road is generally rough and you need to be careful of the ruts created by rain runoff. It can feel like a metal-decked bridge if you get into them. The road is poorly marked, so take the first left after going over Interstate 89 and an immediate right turn. After going past South Pond (on your left), take the next right. Route 65 will lead down the hill and through a farmer's yard to junction at Route 12.

If you choose not to cross the bridge, or discover that the gravel road has recently been graded, which is much like riding on pavement strewn with marbles, return to East Brookfield and continue north on Route 14. You'll be rewarded with the treat of riding through the Williamstown Gulf's twisty passage. In the village of Williamstown, almost across from the junction of Route 64, is **Behind the Scenes,** which serves some of the best fries, pizza, and sub sandwiches around. Route 64 hops over the mountain to Route 12, and a left turn will take you south to where Route 65 junctions.

Route 12 winds and twists down through the Brookfield Gulf and it's a challenging stretch of highway for aggressive riders. From the village of Randolph to the turn onto Camp Brook Road is a pretty tame ride, but that changes once you begin to climb Rochester Mountain. Depending upon your riding inclinations, the next ten miles can be a scenic treat or one that requires every bit of your concentration to remain on the pavement. Fortunately, there's very little traffic other than an occasional local. The 100-mile views from the top, surrounded by birches and pines, are a show-stopper, and the climb is just the way we like 'em—long and curvy!

Middlebury College's Breadloaf Campus on Route 125 is the site of the famous summer Breadloaf Writers Conference and is one of Robert Frost's lasting legacies.

The Plymouth Cheese Company was founded by John Coolidge, the president's father, and the president's son, John Coolidge, operated until his death in 2000. It's now owned and operated by the State of Vermont.

From Rochester, the ride on Route 100 south lasts about a mile before you reach Route 73 west. After making a 90-degree turn at the base of the mountain, Route 73 climbs for five miles to the crest of Brandon Gap at 2,170 feet. The descent offers beautiful glimpses of the Champlain Valley to the west, but the rapid descent, especially when twisting along the gorge of the Neshobe River, will keep you from doing much sightseeing. The descent ends abruptly at the junction of Route 53; the last few miles to camp are an easy meander on this country road.

If you are hungry on either side of the loop, take Route 73 west past Route 53 to Brandon. **Patricia's Restaurant** on Center Street offers fine victuals for lunch and dinner.

Trip 16   Higher Northern Gaps

Distance   *199 miles*

Highlights   *Hairpin corners, mountain passages on gravel roads, scenic vistas, and beautiful valley roads*

The Route from Branbury State Park

0.0   Turn left onto 53 south from Branbury State Park

5.8   Turn left onto Route 73 east

19.3   Turn left onto Route 100 north

20.5   At Rochester, turn right onto Bethel Mountain Road

30.9   Turn left onto Route 12 north

36.3   At Randolph, turn left onto Route 12A north

51.0   At Roxbury, turn left onto Warren Road

56.7   Turn left onto Plunkton Road, which becomes Brook Road; proceed into Warren

59.6   In Warren, turn right onto Main Street

The road over the Lincoln Gap is very much like roads found in the Apennine Mountains of Italy: narrow, steep, and beautiful.

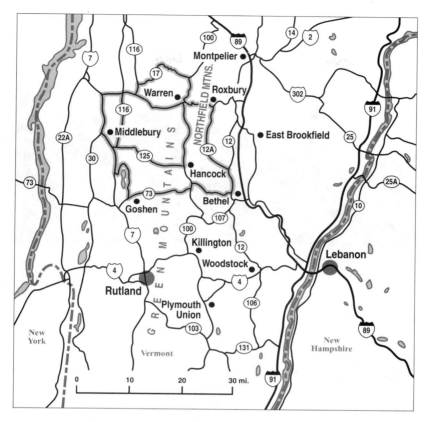

59.9 Turn left onto Route 100, then . . .

60.7 Immediately turn right onto Lincoln Gap Road

71.9 At Rocky Dale, turn right onto combined Routes 116 north and 17 east

73.6 Turn right onto 17 east

89.3 In Irasville (Waitsfield), turn right onto 100 south

109.2 In Hancock, turn right onto Route 125 west

125.2 At East Middlebury, turn right onto Route 7 north

137.2 At New Haven Junction, turn right onto Route 17 east

145.3 At Rocky Dale, turn right onto Lincoln Gap Road

157.3 At Warren, turn left onto Route 100 north

162.8 At Irasville, turn left onto Route 17 west

178.5 Turn left onto combined Routes 17 west/116 south

The view on Route 116 along the base of Lincoln Mountain seen while riding north towards Bristol.

181.2 Turn left onto Route 116 south

192.4 At East Middlebury, turn left onto Route 7 south

195.2 Turn left onto Route 53

198.7 Turn left into Branbury State Park

Start out from the campground taking a 25-mile stretch of road east to Route 12. From Forest Dale, Route 73 climbs along the edge of the gorge formed by the Neshobe River to reach the top of Brandon Gap at 2,170 feet. On the eastern side of the gap, just below the crest, there's a turnoff facing the sheer cliffs on the south side of Mt. Horrid. In the early morning and late evening, you'll probably spot moose in the mud wallows of the pond, while during summer days you might catch a glimpse of peregrine falcons returning to their nesting sites on the cliff face. At the foot of the mountain, the highway makes a 90-degree turn; gravel on the road and an old concrete bridge should make one cautious of this corner.

After crossing the iron bridge over the Second Branch of the White River, turn left and ride into Rochester. Mountain Road begins at the northern end of the bucolic village green and the gas station on the corner would be a good place to top off your fuel tank.

Just a mile and a quarter up Rochester Mountain the road makes a 90-degree turn to the right and continues to climb. The east side, now called Camp Brook Road, is filled with twisty corners until it ends at Route 12.

Follow Route 12 into the village of Randolph, then onto Route 12A, which follows the Third Branch White River, to the small village of Roxbury. Roxbury Gap is one of the prettiest of the Green Mountain gaps, but it's used mostly by locals. These rural roads often change names depending on your direction. In that style, this road is known as Warren Mountain Road on the east side (because it runs west to Warren) and as the Roxbury Gap Road on the west side of the mountain. About a mile and a half from Roxbury it turns to packed gravel that tends to be washboarded in the corners. Just below the crest of the gap on the west side there's a narrow turnoff and a magnificent view of "The Valley." The Appalachian Gap (the lowest point in the range) can be easily identified by its communications tower. Short stretches of the road are paved to prevent it from being washed out, but be careful of gravel in the corners!

At the four-way intersection, take a left and follow Brook Road down to the village of Warren. Either bear left onto Flat Iron Road (it's a street) or turn left at the tiny traffic island in the center of the village. Turn right, dip down, and cross the recently restored covered bridge and up to Route 100. Diagonally across the main highway is the road that goes over Lincoln Gap to Lincoln and Bristol.

The Appalachian Gap is plainly visible as the low point on the horizon as seen from the top of Roxbury Gap. In between lies what locals call simply "The Valley."

In the next 12 miles the road changes to packed gravel twice: a mile-long segment on the east side, and a mile-and-three-quarters section on the west. It reminds me of mountain roads in Europe. At the top of the gap I stopped at the parking area and hiked a portion of the Long Trail, the path that follows the spine of the Green Mountains for the entire length of the state. This is one of the most popular trailheads for weekend hikers; the long expanse to the multiple peaks within the Green Mountains is awesome.

After a long, beautiful descent, much of it along the New Haven River, the road junctions at combined Routes 116 and 17. The last three-tenths of a mile have been along the New Haven Gorge; the New Haven Falls (which swimmers can walk behind) is a popular swimming hole. Turning right, the highway, which runs on top of the Champlain Fault, marks the western boundary of the Green Mountain Range. The wistful feeling brought about by Lincoln Gap lingers until you make a right turn off Route 116 and continue on Route 17 on what is known as the McCullough Turnpike.

An honest road sign on the eastern side of Lincoln Gap.

Looking west from the crest of the Appalachian Gap with Route 17 visible below.

Route 17 is the most challenging 16-mile stretch of road in Vermont. Hairpin (and double hairpin) turns come up without signage—90-degree stuff without warning. The road climbs with alpine dexterity to and through the Appalachian Gap at 2,356 feet. More than a few bikes run the McCullough Turnpike on weekends. Using extreme caution, cross the road and park in the trailhead pulloff to enjoy the views to the west and perhaps to talk with other riders doing the same. The road down the eastern side also has dangerous S turns before *and* after passing the ski area. It's a road you will refer to whenever you play "Oh yeah, well have you ridden . . . !"

(Note: local riders make cautious inspection runs before aggressively tackling these corners. Later, this tour will bring you over the gap from east to west, so memorize the banking and placement of these corners.)

Route 100 at Irasville is just the road you need after the McCullough Turnpike's challenges. Like a racehorse cooling down after the run, it follows the Mad River to its source in the Granville Reservation, then along Alder Meadow Brook to Route 125. Be looking for a paved pulloff on the right as you begin your descent; park and walk past the first waterfall to the beautiful Moss Glen Falls.

At the junction of Route 125 is located the **Old Hancock Hotel,** in which resides the **Vermont Home Bakery.** Three miles up Route 125 is a right-hand turn leading to Texas Falls, should you be inclined to take a break. The climb through this gap is leisurely with just a short stretch of twisting highway on the west side between Ripton and East Middlebury.

In East Middlebury, Route 125 merges with Route 7 north until reaching downtown Middlebury, where it divides and continues west to Crown Point. (See the Lake George Loop.) Route 7 takes you north to New Haven Junction, where a right turn onto 17 east and five miles of undulating highway lead into Bristol.

The quaint appearance of Bristol might be recognized from the 1989 film *The Wizard of Loneliness,* which was set here in "Stebbinsville." It also has a legend of lost treasure said to be buried south of town on a mountainside known as Hell's Half Acre. According to the "Ballad of Old Pocock," Bristol's original name, Simeon Coreser raised a large sum of money to finance his lost treasure diggings. His chief surveyor was his private occultist. His partners, it is told, actually found treasure but Coreser ripped them off with a "field of schemes." The legend of buried treasure lives on, but has yet to be found in Hell's Half Acre.

The Squirrel's Nest Restaurant, on Route 116/17 less than a mile outside of town, is a family-style restaurant where quantity is never debated. Try the sesame chicken or the Big Barrel Breakfast, depending on the time of day and your appetite.

Only four-tenths of a mile beyond the Squirrel's Nest is a right turn onto the road leading through Lincoln Gap, only this time you'll run the gaps in reverse, going west to east through Lincoln to Route 100 in Warren and east to west over the Appalachian Gap. After completing this 35-mile loop you'll ride past the Squirrel's Nest, through the village of Bristol, and to the four-way intersection on the west side of town. Bristol sits on what was the delta of the New Haven River where it entered the Champlain Sea a mere 10,000 years ago. As you ride down the hill you might catch a glimpse of the now distant Lake Champlain.

At the intersection, turn left and follow Route 116 south along the very edge of the Green Mountains to East Middlebury and, just over a half-mile farther, Route 7. This time, take Route 7 south, then Route 53 back to base.

Places of Interest

Brandon

Patricia's Restaurant, 18 Center Street. Phone 802-247-3223. Daily 11:00 a.m. to 9:00 p.m. Good burgers, soups, and daily specials. $$

Bristol

The Squirrel's Nest Restaurant, Route 116. Phone 802-453-6042. Daily, 5:00 a.m. to 9:00 p.m. Family dining. Say hi to Jay, the owner. Sesame chicken, Big Barrel Breakfast. $$

Hancock

Old Hancock Hotel, Corner of Routes 100 and 125. No phone. Daily 7:00 a.m. to 8:00 p.m. Cob-smoked meats, down-home cooking. $$

Woodstock

Billings Farm and Museum, open May 1 through October 31, 10:00 a.m. to 5:00 p.m. 802-457-2355. www.billingsfarm.org

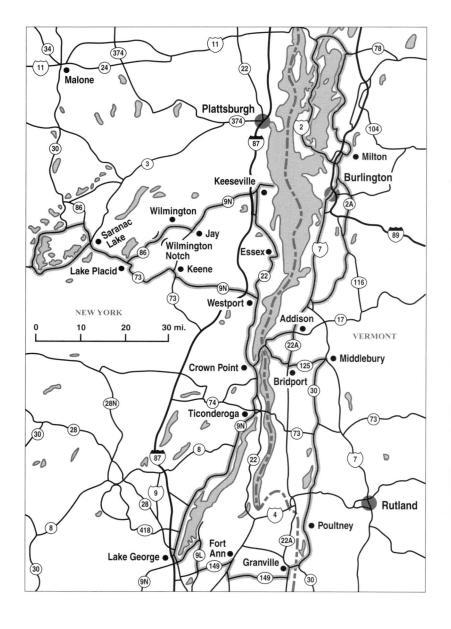

Circumnavigating the Lakes

This journey encompasses the beauty and adventure of the three largest lakes—Champlain, George, and Placid—between the Adirondack and Green Mountain ranges. Many of the highlights in this chapter are geological in nature (pun intended). This part of the Northeast offers challenging roads, historic sites to visit, and natural scenery to enjoy.

I chose the **Crown Point State Park** in New York for home base. Sitting in view of the Champlain Bridge, it afforded me an opportunity to camp by the lake with easy access to Vermont. Stay in the waterfront lean-to if possible. The lake is down a steep embankment in front of the lean-to that leads to a very private flat rock beach of Crown Point limestone. Otherwise the campground is fairly open.

Lake Placid as viewed from Whiteface Mountain is framed by the "Ancient Adirondack Mountains."

Trip 17 Lake George Loop

Distance *156 miles without sidetrips*

Highlights *Scenic lake and mountain views and points of historic interest. There are also three nice stretches of highway for pure motorcycle riding pleasure.*

The Route from Crown Point Campground

0.0 Turn left exiting the Crown Point Campground

3.6 Turn left onto Routes 9N south/22 south

7.2 In Crown Point, bear to the left

The view looking east toward Lake George from above Bolton Landing is breathtaking.

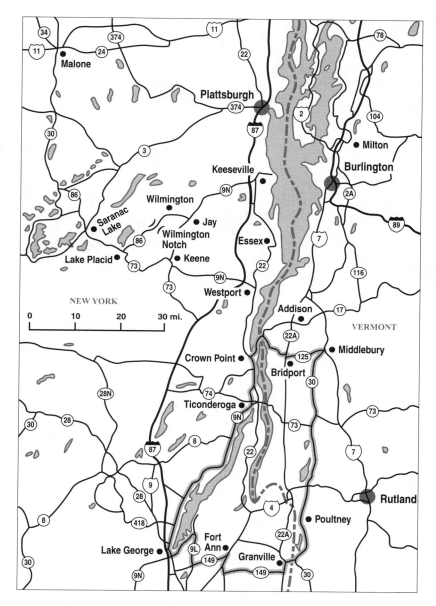

14.9 Proceed straight on Route 9N south. (For a side trip to Fort Ticonderoga, turn left here onto Routes 74 east/22 south)

15.7 Bear to the right to proceed on Route 9N south. Proceed around the rotary, then turn right onto Montcalm west for side trip to Mt. Defiance and Fort Ticonderoga

Taking a paddlewheeler tour is another way to cruise Lake George.

52.7 In Lake George, bear left onto Canada Street (combined Routes 9N south and 9 south)

53.4 Proceed on combined Routes 9N and 9. (For an alternate route along the east side of Lake George, turn left here onto Lake Street toward the steamship docks and Route 9L)

54.6 Where Routes 9 and 9N split, proceed straight on Route 9 south

57.2 Turn left onto Route 149 east

64.7 Proceed straight through the intersection of Route 9L

72.0 In Fort Ann, turn right onto Routes 149 east/4 south

73.9 Where Routes 4 and 149 split, bear left and proceed on Route 149; *caution advised*

82.0 At Hartford, turn left onto Routes 149 east and 40 west

82.4 Turn right on Route 149 east

88.1 At South Granville, bear left to stay on Route 149 east

90.0 In Granville, turn left onto Routes 149 east/22 north. *Immediately* bear right to stay on Route 149 east

90.8 Bear right to stay on Route 149

92.9 Turn left onto Route 30

02.7 In Poultney, observe *caution* for a dangerous 90-degree left turn

102.9 Turn right and proceed on Route 30

138.9 At Middlebury, turn left onto Route 125 west

147.3 At Bridport, turn right onto Routes 125 west and 22A north

147.7 Turn left on Route 125 west

155.3 Proceed straight when Route 125 junctions at Route 17

156.2 Turn left into the Crown Point campground

The run from the site of the Crown Point fortifications to that of the more famous **Fort Ticonderoga** is a quick 15-mile ride south on Routes 9N and 22. "Fort Ti" is a must for all Revolutionary War buffs and offers expansive views of Lake Champlain. The easiest way to reach the fort is by turning left at the intersection of Route 74 and following it west; the entrance is well marked. But to truly understand its strategic importance one must first visit Mt. Defiance. At the small rotary, make a 180-degree turn and follow Montcalm west into the center of downtown Ticonderoga, then a right onto Champlain Street and the next left (well marked) leading to the Mt. Defiance Toll Road. From the summit at 853 feet you can look down on the fortifications and enjoy spectacular views of the lakes. With its guns facing down on Fort Ticonderoga, you get a feeling for the historic battles that took place here.

South of Ticonderoga the road gets a little twisty as you approach Hague and receive your first views of Lake George. The road dips down to some vicious curves on the very edge of the lake as you enter the village proper. Exactly six miles beyond the junction of Route 8 in Hague are two turnoffs along the lake. *Stop.* These are the best vantage points for photo ops on this loop.

Immediately beyond the turnoffs the road heads away from the lake and twists and turns as it climbs into the Tongue Mountain Range. For the next nine miles Route 9N becomes motorcycle heaven as it runs through the wilderness, offering one of the best rides in the region.

Bolton Landing can be a busy little town during the height of the tourist season, but because of this it offers a wide variety of places to eat. Try a late morning breakfast at **Bolton Beans** or **Frank's Breakfast and Lunch** or wait until reaching Lake George. There are plenty of places to eat in the next eleven miles and your choice may be dictated as much by traffic as any other factor.

The village of Lake George is touristy with all the trappings, not that you mind getting trapped now and then. In early June the **Americade** touring rally draws 50,000 motorcyclists to a village that has a winter population of less than 500 residents and you really have to experience it to visualize this village packed with bikes of all descriptions. A different mode of seeing the town and lakeshore is by steamship out of the harbor. Opposite the steamship docks is Fort Henry which protected the southern end of the lake.

(See Side Trip to French Mountain)

On the southern end of the village Route 9N heads west, but you want to continue straight on Route 9 for another 2.5 miles to the junction of Route 149. **The Great Escape Fun Park** is the largest amusement park in New York, with more than 100 rides and attractions. Although this park is listed as being in Lake George, you actually have to continue south on Route 9 almost to Glens Falls to find it. Once on Route 149, you'll be happy to bring your steed up to a comfortable 55 mph once again.

South of the village of Fort Ann, Route 149 crosses the Champlain Canal and the open landscape with undulating hills becomes an enjoyable ride with plenty of tight corners lurking just behind the next slight rise. Beyond Fort Ann, where Routes 4 and 149 split, exercise great caution as you make the left onto Route 149, since northbound traffic on Route 4 is fast and your visibility to that traffic is poor. In Granville you might notice that almost every building has a slate shingled roof. This is the heart of the "slate belt" where quarries produce the gray, green, purple, and red sedimentary stone that was traditionally used for roofing slate, but which now finds more use as floor and patio tiles. You'll notice piles of waste rock and the giant boom cranes of Douglas fir positioned over active quarries from here to Castleton, Vermont.

Riding north on Route 30, the highway gets squeezed between Lake St. Catherine and St. Catherine Mountain—literarily the western edge of the Taconic Mountains—before winding into Poultney. Then it's a straight shot north along the shore of Lake Bomoseen and then along the Champlain Valley, which offers dramatic views of the Adirondacks on your left and the Green Mountains on your right. Rubbernecking is allowed because Route 30 is a smooth and easy ride the rest of the way to Middlebury.

➡ Side Trip to French Mountain

Turn left onto Lake Street, past the steamship docks and Million Dollar Beach to Route 9L. Taking a left, this road follows the east side of the lake to go around French Mountain and then south to join Route 149.   ■

Bolton Beans, a gassing up spot, is popular among riders cruising through Bolton Landing on Lake George.

Most places have their own local lore and Lake Bomoseen is no exception. In the middle of the lake you might notice a small island, Neshobe, which used to be a popular summer retreat for Hollywood celebrities during the 1930s and '40s. Legend had it that one of these residents finally got tired of the autograph seekers trespassing on the island and one day when a boat load of these tourists disembarked Harpo Marx was lying in ambush. When they were close enough he charged from the underbrush screaming, naked, and painted blue from head to toe. This solved the problem for the rest of the season.

Middlebury is a college town with all the associated food, drink, and resting places. **Woody's** is a place to get some good food and see a lively cross-section of the town's residents. If you're into live steeds (if you brought this book I assume you are already into the iron variety), the University of Vermont's famous Morgan Horse farm is just five miles north of Middlebury in Weybridge. (If you take Route 23 to Weybridge, just continue to Route 17 and then turn west to return to the Crown Point campsite.) Route 125 heads west across the undulating Champlain Valley, briefly joining Route 22A, before bringing you back to the Champlain Bridge and hence to home base on the other side.

Trip 18 Lake Placid Loop

Distance *193 miles without sidetrips or alternate routes*

Highlights *Mountains and lake views, twisty roads, and an optional ferry crossing. Also, sidetrips up Whiteface Mountain and to Ausable Chasm*

The Route from Crown Point Campground

0.0 Turn left exiting the Crown Point Campground

3.6 Turn right onto Routes 9N north/22 north

17.6 At Westport, bear left proceeding on Route 9N north

Rainbow Falls at Ausable Chasm viewed from the Route 9 bridge over the Ausable River.

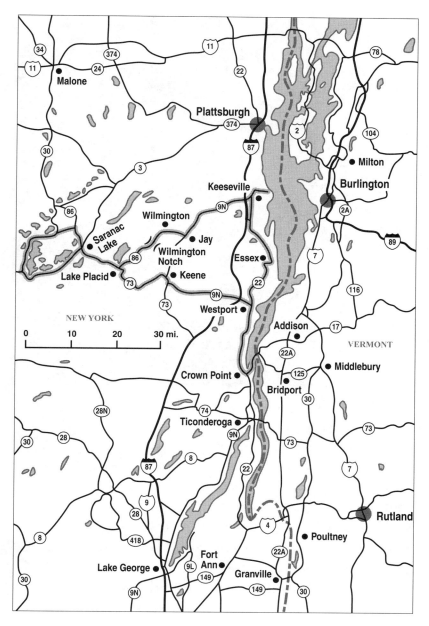

26.0 In Elizabethtown, turn left on combined Routes 9 south/9N north

26.5 Turn right on Route 9N north

36.5 Turn right on Routes 9N north/73 north

The climb up Whiteface Mountain is a popular motorcycle destination. This collection of bikes represents several separate groups of riders who have chosen to take the elevator to the summit.

38.4 At Keene, bear left on Route 73 north

52.4 In Lake Placid, turn left onto Route 86 west

62.0 In Saranac Lake, where Route 86 bears right, keep left on River Street, which becomes Route 3 west after two blocks; follow Route 3 west

77.4 Turn right onto Route 30 north

91.6 At Lake Clear Junction, proceed straight onto Route 186 east

95.5 Near Harrietstown, turn right onto Route 86 east

100.1 In Saranac Lake, turn left onto Routes 3 east/86 east for one block

100.2 Turn right on Route 86 east

100.6 Bear left (River Street is on your right) on Route 86 east

110.2 In Lake Placid, proceed straight on Route 86 at the junction of Route 73

122.2 At Wilmington, turn right to continue this tour on Route 86 east, or turn left onto Route 431 for the side trip up Whiteface Mountain

127.2 At Jay, turn left onto Route 9N north

144.7 At Keeseville, turn right onto Routes 22 south/9 south, or bear left onto 9 north to Ausable Chasm sidetrip

149.2 Turn left to stay on Route 22 south

162.2 In Essex, stop at the ferry dock to take the alternate route back to Crown Point

175.2 In Westport, turn left on Routes 22 south/9N south

189.2 Turn left onto Route 8 east toward the Champlain Bridge

192.8 Turn right into the campground

This loop is high drama from the beginning run along the shore of Lake Champlain on through the climb into the Adirondacks, an outstanding loop around Saranac Lake, the piercing of Wilmington Notch, and the conquering of Whiteface Mountain. Once on combined Routes 22 north and 9N, the highway hugs the shoreline affording great views of Vermont on the opposite shore. Just north of the village of Port Henry, you can look over your shoulder and see the arched silver bridge and the old ruins on the Crown Point peninsula. However, in the spring and fall the difference in temperature between the air and the lake water frequently creates heavy fog, obscuring these beautiful views.

At the northern end of the downtown district in Westport the routes divide, with 9N bearing to the left. Four miles farther, the highway passes under Interstate 87 and the views of the mountains to the west promise exciting riding to come. With the Adirondacks rising directly ahead, the view becomes ever more teasing as you approach Elizabethtown, where Route 9N briefly merges with Route 9 before turning west and winding its way through the mountains for the next ten miles.

On the long descent to Keene, the view of Lake Placid is obstructed by a formidable barrier of the next range of mountains, but Route 73 loops around Owl's Head Mountain and begins to climb a narrow passage through them. For several miles, the highway offers a very necessary truck-passing lane so you can get by the long lines of recreational vehicles that crawl through this pass on summer weekends. The road skims along the edge of the long, narrow Cascade Lake and the numerous pulloff areas are the most pleasant you'll find for many miles. Just beyond these small lakes are parking areas for the numerous trailheads that lead into the Mt. Van Hoevenburg State Recreational Area and to Round Lake; be alert for turning traffic and hikers.

The first indication that you're approaching Lake Placid will be the towers of the Olympic ski jump rising above the tree line. This small village is an international destination and the center of tourism in the Adirondack region. If you've been on the road too long and need a little culture, Lake Placid is a place to recharge your civilization batteries. There are plenty of places to eat and shop in the busy downtown area, which is designed to resemble a quaint alpine European village. There are plenty of commercial American-style offerings along Route 86 as you leave the village en route to Saranac Lake.

The loop around Saranac Lake is fun, with Route 3 offering long straights with some dipsy-doodles in the road. Route 30 is challenging—especially around **Fish Creek Pond**—with its 90-degree turns and twists providing excitement to contrast with the scenic beauty. The degree of difficulty, as always, is determined by your speed. The state parks on this loop (for example, Fish Creek Pond) offer swimming and camping facilities on the lake and are great places for a picnic or to rest and savor your experience. Route 186 and Route 86 bring you back into the village of Saranac Lake where, in the middle of town, the park and picnic tables along the shore of Flower Lake offer another option for an idyllic break after hours on the road.

The Castle on Whiteface Mountain adds an exclamation point to a fantastic summit assault.

▶ Side Trip to Whiteface Mountain

If it's a clear day, you'll want to take the 15-mile side trip to the top of White-face Mountain. Route 431 is also called the Veterans Memorial Highway and will take you to 4,460 feet above sea level. The tollhouse is only three miles from the intersection and you'll want to check the weather conditions at the top of the mountain before plunking down your five bucks per person. The next five miles of pavement are twisty and filled with frost heaves and dips as it climbs over 2,300 feet in elevation. There are numerous places to turn off and park along the way, including the stunning overlook of Lake Placid and the Wilmington Turn, which at 4,300 feet affords an incredible view of Lake Champlain and Vermont. From the upper parking area an elevator transports visitors to the summit at 4,867 feet for unparalleled views of the Adirondack region. On the way back down the mountain you can practice your swerving techniques against the mogul-like frost heaves. If you're economizing, the road just below the tollhouse to the Atmospheric Sciences Research Center (State University of New York at Albany) provides similar views, but at lower elevations. Be nice, though, since the road to the testing center is not a public right-of-way.

Route 86 junctions at Route 9N in the upper Ausable Valley. Taking a left turn, follow the East Branch Ausable River to where it is joined by the West Branch in Au Sable Forks (Note: the town is spelled as two words; the river as one), then farther downstream to Keeseville. When you pass under Interstate 87, only a mile and a half remains of Route 9N and a decision whether or not to take a short side trip to visit Ausable Chasms. To continue south on combined Routes 22 and 9 requires a hard right turn and crossing the bridge over the Ausable River; bearing left on Route 9 leads to Ausable Chasm. ■

Following Route 86 east you once again go through the village of Lake Placid and soon are following the West Branch Ausable River into the mountains on a very twisty road. The valley keeps getting narrower mile after mile until finally there's barely enough room for both the river and the road as you ride along **High Falls Gorge** in the middle of Wilmington Notch. After passing the Wilmington Campground and the entrance to the Whiteface Mountain Ski Area, the valley widens a little and you'll reach the four-way intersection of Routes 86, 19, and 431.

(See Side Trip to Whiteface Mountain)

(See Side Trip to Ausable Chasm)

(See Side Trip to Essex)

➡ Side Trip to Ausable Chasm

Ausable Chasm is a box canyon cut through sandstone by the Ausable River. Located only a mile north on Route 9, this scenic wonder has been a popular tourist destination for decades. The canyon is privately owned property and a fee is charged for access to the maintained walkways within it, but the lofty view of Rainbow Falls from the bridge over the Ausable River (Route 9) is free.

The best find was **Harold's Bar.** Just follow the walkway out behind the tourist center, across the old bridge by the dam. Harold will provide a nonstop history since the thirties, a few times over, in the space of a cold drink. It's less expensive than the tourist center, the entertainment by Harold is free, and the horseshoe pits are beside the dam.

Two ferry crossings offer alternate modes and roads back to Crown Point. The first, just five miles down Route 373 from Ausable Chasm, crosses from Port Kent to Burlington ($5 for bike and rider and $3.50 for a passenger) and the forty-five-minute crossing is the most scenic ferry ride in New England. From Burlington, take Route 7 south to Route 22A at Vergennes to Route 17 west. The second—and, I think, better if Burlington is not your destination—is the ferry from Essex, N.Y. to Charlotte, Vermont.

Following Route 9 back to Route 22 in Keeseville, you'll ride parallel to I-87 for a few miles until, at one of the interstate highway exits, Route 22 makes an abrupt left turn and runs southeast towards the lakeshore. Vistas of the Green Mountains are plainly visible while riding down the hill, and the V-shaped notch in those mountains marks the location of the village of Bristol. (See the Higher Northern Gaps tour.) After going through the beautiful village of Willsboro and following the lakeshore, you'll arrive at Essex and the Champlain Transportation Company's ferry dock for the crossing to Charlotte. The Champlain Transportation Company is the oldest continuous operating shipping company in the world, beginning service on the lake with their first steamship, the *Vermont,* in 1809. This was the second commercial steamship in existence (Fulton's *North River of Clermont* was first in 1807), built and operated by the original pilot of the *North River.* Essex is a charming little town in which to eat. The **Old Dock Restaurant** is surrounded on three sides by water, just within view of the ferry. Don't bother to count the number of ferries you missed. ∎

Sweeping curves and panoramic views make the climb up Whiteface Mountain a worthwhile side trip.

➡ Side Trip to Essex

The ferry, which runs every half-hour, is a pretty 30-minute ride with the Adirondacks and the Green Mountains as opposing backdrops. It's inexpensive—$4.25 for the bike and rider; $2.50 for a passenger—and it provides a break from two-wheeled transportation. (Be sure to put the bike in first gear on the centerstand and don't take it off until the ferry bumps the dock for the last time.) When you disembark, proceed on Route F-4 to Route 7 south, then Route 22A south to Route 17 east and back to Crown Point.

From Essex, the highway turns away from the lake and runs inland before turning and meandering across the agricultural landscape back to Westport. Here joining Route 9N south, it's just an 18-mile run back to the Crown Point campsite. The views of Vermont are just as spectacular when traveling south as when riding north, and if your morning ride began in the fog, this late afternoon return will reward you with previously unseen panoramic views. The view of the Champlain Bridge and the old fortifications of Crown Point are clearly visible just across Bulwagga Bay, but it's another 13-miles before pulling into the campground and the end of today's ride. ∎

Trip 19 Grand Isle Loop

Distance *174 miles without side trips*

Highlights *Spectacular lake and mountain panoramic vistas are the primary feature of this loop, but twisting country roads and a ride through the city of Burlington are two others*

The Route from Crown Point Campground

0.0 Turn right out of the Crown Point campsite and proceed over the bridge and onto Route 17 east

9.2 At Addison, turn left onto Route 22A north

16.6 At Vergennes, turn left onto Route 7 north

This statue of Samuel de Champlain on Isle La Motte commemerates his exploration of his namesake Lake Champlain and his befriending the Native Americans who helped him.

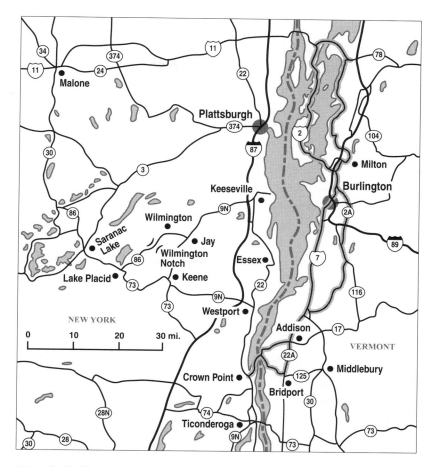

36.8 In Burlington, at the small traffic island on the north end of Shelburne Road (Route 7), turn right and proceed up the hill on Ledge Road

37.1 Proceed straight through the traffic light onto Prospect Street

38.4 Turn right onto Colchester Avenue

38.8 Proceed straight through the traffic light with East Avenue on your right

39.3 Proceed straight through every set of traffic lights on Routes 2 west/7 north

40.6 You'll know you are on the correct route as you pass by Exit 16 of Interstate 89; continue on Route 2 west/7 north

43.9 At Colchester, and the junction of Route 2A, continue straight on Routes 2 west/7 north

46.9 Near Chimney Corner, turn left on Route 2 west

74.4 Turn left for the side trip on Route 129 to Isle La Motte

79.8 Near Arlburg, turn right onto Route 78 east

89.7 At Swanton, bear right onto Route 36 south (Lake Street), then turn right

100.7 At St. Albans, bear right onto Georgia Shore Road

101.0 Turn right

102.8 Turn right to stay on Georgia Shore Road

109.7 Turn left onto Lake Road

116.9 Near Milton, turn right onto Route 7 south

123.2 At Chimney Corner (near Exit 17 of Interstate 89), continue straight on Routes 7 south/2 east

126.4 At Colchester, bear left onto Route 2A south

140.1 Near Hinesburg, Route 116 joins Route 2A

143.3 At Hinesburg, proceed straight onto Silver Street

148.6 Turn right onto Monkton Road (toward Moncton Ridge and Moncton Boro)

157.8 Near Vergennes, proceed straight through the intersection of Route 7

158.2 At Vergennes, turn left onto Route 22A south (Main Street)

164.7 At Addison, turn right onto Route 17 west

172.8 Cross the Champlain Bridge at Chimney Point

173.9 Turn left into the Crown Point Campground

This loop is the most scenic of the three in the Lakes Journey. The biggest challenge here is to keep from getting into trouble while you gawk at Lake Champlain, the wildlife, and the mountains. Burlington is a college town with dozens of exceptional places to eat in the revitalized downtown area, so you might plan to stop and have dinner here before finishing the last leg of this loop.

This journey begins by riding over the Champlain Bridge and continuing on Route 17 across the lush grasslands of Addison County. Route 22A then leads north to Vergennes, the smallest, and third oldest, incorporated city in the United States.

Coming into the city the highway crosses the falls on the Otter Creek and from the bridge you can glance down at the large pool where Benedict Arnold's fleet of boats was built for his famous engagement against the British fleet in 1776. Commander MacDonough's fleet of ships, which defeated the British navy at the Battle of Plattsburg in 1814, was also built in this pool at the foot of the falls eight miles from the shores of Lake Champlain. For a better view of the falls, take the first left after crossing the bridge onto MacDonough Drive and down to the parking area.

Route 7 is one of the busiest highways in Vermont and the ride from Vergennes to Burlington will be at a rapid pace until reaching the village of Shelburne, home to the famous **Shelburne Museum.** If you have a spare day you might consider coming back and enjoying one of the best displays of Americana in the country.

The ride through Burlington can be a trying experience since Shelburne Road (Route 7) is several miles of strip malls and turning traffic. At the northern end of Shelburne Road is a very small traffic island and you need to

Isle La Motte is not only the site of St. Anne's Shrine and the landing place of Samuel D. Champlain, it's also the source of the gray limestone used as the facade of our nation's capitol building, the Brooklyn Bridge, and Radio City Music Hall.

The Hyde Log cabin, in the village of Grand Isle on Route 2, is one of the oldest surviving log cabins in the United States and is worth a brief visit.

decide which streets to take before reaching it. To ride into downtown Burlington for breakfast, bear to your left around the traffic island and then immediately bear right to continue on St. Paul Street. To follow Route 7 north, bear to right onto South Willard Street and proceed to the traffic light at the intersection of Main Street. However, turn right (don't follow the signs for Routes 2 west and 7 north) and go up the hill two blocks to the next traffic light, then turn left either at the light or the very next street, and ride along the green in the heart of the University of Vermont campus. At the end of the green, turn right and follow Colchester Avenue into the city of Winooski and out the other side through Colchester. Another more scenic option with less traffic is to turn right at the traffic circle and climb the hill on Ledge Street and then through the Champlain College and University of Vermont campuses on North Prospect Street to the UVM green. There's plenty to see, but if the traffic is heavy do what local riders do: take I-189 from Shelburne Road to I-89 north; then the second Winooski exit (16) onto Route 7 north or Exit 17 onto Route 2 west at Chimney Corners.

The fun begins again at Chimney Corners. Route 2 crosses the Lamoille River and then runs through the river's delta and its wetlands (Sandbar Wildlife Management Area) to cross the narrow causeway to the island of South Hero. (Note: It is South Hero Island, Grand Isle County, and both South Hero and Grand Isle townships.) In the village of Grand Isle is the **Hyde Log Cabin,** the oldest surviving log cabin in the United States and still in original condition. A drawbridge connects South Hero and North Hero over a narrow channel and double bay called "The Gut." President Franklin D. Roosevelt often boasted that, as a teenager, he was one of only two civilians who could navigate one of the great Champlain steamships through this dangerous passage. Route 2 goes past the summer home of the famous Royal Lipizzan Stallions, and through the village of North Hero where you might just catch the international bagpipe competition that takes place here for two weeks every August. Through it all are rolling vistas and beautiful views of the Adirondack Mountains to the west.

Just after crossing the bridge to Alburg, which feels like another of the Champlain Islands but is a peninsula connected to Canada, is the turn onto Route 129. This side trip takes you across the peninsula and a short causeway to Isle La Motte. This island is famous for its gray limestone, which was used for the facade of the U.S. Capitol building, Radio City Music Hall, and the Brooklyn Bridge, to name just a few. It's also known for having the oldest fossil coral reefs on the planet. This small rural island is also where the famous explorer Samuel de Champlain first set foot on Vermont soil in 1609, the same site that became Vermont's first permanent settlement, Fort St. Anne in 1666. The beautiful **St. Anne Shrine** now marks the location of the old fort and a statue of Samuel de Champlain, sculpted at Canada's EXPO '67, graces the shoreline. Picnic tables make this an ideal place to take a break before continuing your journey.

Return to Route 2 north via Route 129 and continue to Route 78 east, to the mainland. Route 2 cuts a swath through the wetlands of the Missisquoi National Wildlife Refuge (a major North American breeding area for Great Blue Herons) as it follows the river of the same name. As you begin to enter the village of Swanton, immediately before crossing the Missisquoi River, bear to the right onto Route 36. Most of this route is along the shore of the lake and on a pleasant afternoon offers one of the most scenic rides in northern Vermont.

Just as you reach St. Albans Bay, about ten miles south of Swanton, you will see signs for Kill Kare State Park. The right turn (Hathaway Point Road) makes you wonder where the road leads. *Do it!* The park is at the end of a small peninsula with picnic tables and BBQ set-ups, and is a perfect escape from "NumButt." If you are even more adventurous, the park service offers launch rides, people and gear only, to Burton Island and Wood's Island State Parks for camping.

Burton Island has all the modern camping conveniences, while Wood's Island is limited to five parties and a "carry out what you carry in" policy for this primitive wilderness setting.

Back on Route 36 south, exactly seven-tenths of a mile farther and at the end of the St. Albans Town Park and the beginning of the village of St. Albans Bay, bear right onto the Georgia Shore Road. Route 36 leads into St. Albans, but this local road follows the shoreline south. It's an incredibly beautiful ride and you'll be glad you made the effort. There is a mile-and-a-half stretch of gravel road about six miles south of St. Albans Bay, easy to negotiate with minimal dust envelopment. The pavement makes a left turn and becomes Lake Road as it leaves the shoreline (going straight takes you back onto gravel and is posted as being a DEAD END). Lake Road takes you to Arrowhead Lake in Milton and the first few miles of this narrow road wind and undulate across a rural landscape before turning into suburban tract housing once you cross the interstate highway.

Route 7 is the bank of the Arrowhead Lake and after crossing the bridge you're in the village of Milton. Chittenden County was one of the fastest growing areas in the United States in the mid-1990s and is still ranked one of the best places to live in the United States. However, the price has been the conversion of prime farmland into urban sprawl. The most scenic route, which is also the fastest and has the least traffic is, ironically, Interstate 89 from Chimney Corners to Tafts Corners in Williston (14.9 miles from Exit 17 to Exit 12 and Route 2A). Otherwise, Routes 7 south and 2 east join in Chimney Corners and continue through the cities of Winooski and Burlington. Alternate Route 2A (13.8 miles total) begins just north of the village of Colchester and runs through Essex Junction and Tafts Corners in Williston to the junction at Route 116 in St. George. *Caution:* beware of oncoming traffic when bearing left onto Route 2A opposite the Colchester Plaza. The first and last few miles of Route 2A are pleasant, but be prepared for a considerable amount of turning traffic in Essex Junction and the vast commercial area known as Tafts Corners.

If you chose to ride through Burlington, stay on combined Routes 7 south and 2 east through Winooski and continue up the hill—don't follow the signs for Routes 7 and 2, which require bearing right on Riverside Avenue—until reaching the first traffic lights, then turn left onto East Street (follow the signs to I-89), then left onto Williston Road (Route 2 south). You'll see the bright yellow sign for **Al's French Frys** on your left after the fifth set

Looking north across the Champlain Valley from the junction of Routes 17 and 22A in Addison with Mt. Philo visible on the horizon.

of traffic lights. If you're a fry meister this is the place to stop! Turn right at the seventh set of traffic lights onto Route 116 (Hinesburg Road).

Route 116, whether you picked it up in Burlington or in St. George by taking the alternate Route 2A, leads south to the village of Hinesburg. In the village, the road takes a sweeping 90-degree turn to the left, but continues straight onto what is known as Monkton Road (don't be confused by the signs identifying it as Silver Street). These 15 miles of rolling farmland heaven, with some sweeping turns, are a direct shot into Vergennes. When Monkton Road reaches the traffic lights at Route 7 proceed straight to Route 22A in the city. Then you can either follow the route ridden earlier in the day back to camp, or take the third right after crossing the bridge over the falls onto Panton Road (signs clearly mark this turn to Button Bay State Park, Basin Harbor Club, and the Lake Champlain Maritime Museum). Continue straight to Panton (don't turn right onto Basin Harbor Road) and then south to rejoin Route 17 west just north of D.A.R. State Park and back to base.

Places of Interest

NEW YORK

Ausable Chasm

Harold's Bar, three-minute walk behind Ausable Chasm entrance across the old bridge by the dam. Phone 518-834-9907. Daily, noon 'til Harold decides to close. Harold is always there with a story behind Ausable Chasm. Horseshoes, cold drinks, and picnic tables. $

Crown Point

Crown Point State Park, at Lake Champlain Bridge, R.D. #1, Crown Point 12928. Phone 518-597-3603. Open daily mid-April to mid-October. Grab the waterfront lean-to if you can.

Essex

Old Dock Restaurant, Route 22. Phone 518-963-4232. Daily lunch and dinner mid-May through mid-October. Center of town, casual, outdoor bar and grill. Reservations. $$$

Saranac Lake

Fish Creek Pond State Park, Route 30 north. Phone 518-891-4560. All the amenities plus beach and lake swimming. Reservations accepted.

The Champlain Bridge at Crown Point is one of only two bridges across the lake. The remaining trans-lake traffic is managed by ferry boats.

Pontiac Restaurant, 100 Main Street (opposite the Hotel Saranac). Phone 518-891-5200. Sunday 10:00 a.m. to 5:00 p.m.; Monday 10:00 to 3:00 p.m; Tuesday to Thursday 10:30 a.m. to 9:00 p.m. Light foods and sandwiches; fresh, delicious food and the wait is worth it. $$

Ticonderoga

Fort Ticonderoga, Route 74, Ticonderoga. Phone 518-585-2821. www.fort-ticonderoga.org. Open early May to late October. Admission charged. This National Historic Landmark is a living history museum with colonial reenactments taking place on special dates.

VERMONT

South Burlington

Al's French Frys, 1251 Williston Road (Route 2). Phone 802-862-9203. Daily 11:00 a.m. to 11:00 p.m. Superb French fries and all fried foods. $$

Grand Isle

North Hero State Park, Route 2. Phone 802-372-8727. Open May through mid-October. On Lake Champlain, the campground is excellent, well kept, available with firewood, BBQs, and beach.

Isle La Motte

St. Anne's Shrine, Isle La Motte. Phone 802-928-3362. www.sse.org. Cafeteria overlooking the lake is open daily and picnic tables and the beach are open to all.

Middlebury

Woody's Restaurant, 5 Bakery Lane. Phone 802-388-4182. Daily, 11:30 a.m. to midnight. Casual dining and drinking, outside decks, art deco interior, innovative menu. $$

St. Albans Bay

Burton Island State Park, St. Albans Bay. Phone 802-524-6353. Rates, $15–$22 per night. Open mid-May through mid-October. 42 campsites included 26 lean-tos and most are along the lakeshore. Hot showers, flush toilets, and more. Ferry ($) leaves from Kill Kare State Park.

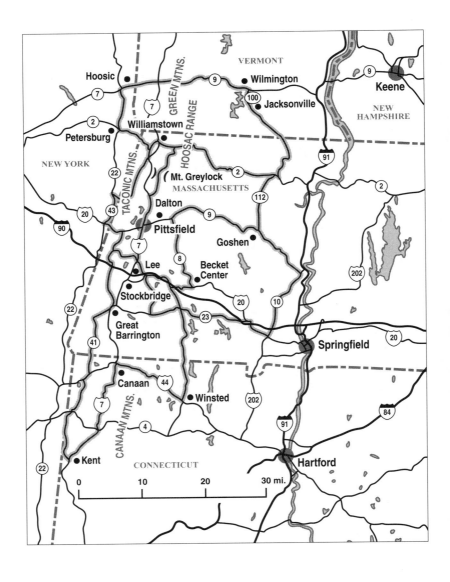

Cruisin' the Berkshires

The Berkshires are a range of low mountains located for the most part in western Massachusetts. Their borders extend north to Vermont, west to New York State, south to Connecticut and east to Massachusetts' Pioneer Valley. The rides set out here are designed to avoid traffic congestion and introduce you to the wide expanse of rolling hills, rivers, and lakes, while swinging by some of the more interesting sights in the region.

In summer, the region hosts a vast assortment of entertainment: theater and art at the Clark Art Museum in Williamstown, dance at Jacob's Pillow Dance Festival in Becket, and the Norman Rockwell museum in Stockbridge. Spring and fall are less populated; during those seasons you'll find less congested roads and off-season rates for everything, except during the first two weeks of October when fall colors bring people from all over the country to view nature's spectacle.

For this journey, I created my base camp at the **October Mountain State Forest,** in Lee, near Lenox, Mass. Lenox is centrally located with a variety of places to stay, ranging from posh well-known inns to motels and campgrounds. From downtown Lenox at the merging of Routes 183 and 7A, it's 6.6 miles to the campsite. Go east on Route 183 (Walker Street), crossing Route 7 to the 5-way intersection. Turn left on East Street (north); right onto Housatonic Street to Lenox Station (4-way intersection); right (south) on Chrystal Street; first left, cross the railroad tracks, left onto Valley Street to Woodland Road and the entrance to the campsite. Note that from the intersection of Walker Street and East Street, Blantyre Road leads directly to Route 20 by the Cranwell Resort and Golf Club in Lee.

The best way to get to the Berkshires from Boston is the Mohawk Trail (Route 2). About 140 miles in length from Boston to the Berkshires, Route 2 starts as a four-lane highway near Boston and, west of Orange, Mass., narrows to two-lane twisties, scenic views and overlooks, and one hairpin turn.

From New York, grab U.S. Highway 684 north to the intersection of N.Y. Route 22 north. Hang a right at Haviland, N.Y. to Conn. Route 37 north to Conn. Route 7 north. This route is direct, with sufficient back road content to keep your interest, and picks up the Southern Berkshire loop. You may want to go home that way.

Trip 20   Northern Berkshire Loop

Distance *183 miles*

Highlights *Rural roads with plenty of tight curves, a climb to the summit of the highest mountain in Massachusetts, and interesting places to stop.*

The Route from Downtown Lenox

0.0 From the intersection of Main Street (Route 7A) and Walker Street (Route 183) in Lenox, proceed east on Walker Street

0.2 Bear left to stay on Route 183 east

1.0 Bear right onto Lee Road

The Bridge of Flowers, which began as a simple civic project, has become a regional destination.

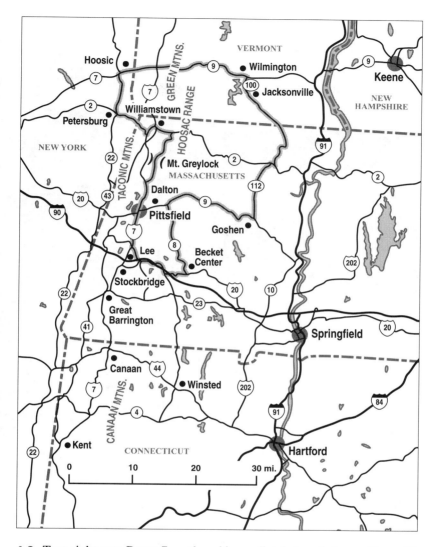

1.2 Turn right onto Route 7 south and immediately bear left onto Route 20 east

17.6 Near Becket Center, turn left onto Route 8 north

36.5 At Dalton, turn right onto Route 9 east

59.4 At Goshen, turn left onto Route 112 north

92.8 At Jacksonville, Vermont, bear right onto Route 100 north

99.5 Near Wilmington, bear left to continue on Route 9 west

The Bridge of Flowers in Shelburne Falls is an ingenious use of the old abandoned railroad bridge.

129.1 Beyond Hoosic, New York, turn left onto Route 22 south

136.7 At Petersburg, New York, turn left onto Route 2 east

146.3 Near Williamstown, turn left onto Routes 2 east/7 north

148.5 In Williamstown, bear right and continue on Route 2 east

152.8 Near North Adams, turn right onto Notch Road

160.6 Turn right onto Rockwell Road, OR turn left to proceed to the summit parking lots

168.2 In Lanesborough, bear right onto Greylock Road

168.6 Turn left onto North Main Street

169.4 Turn right onto Route 7 south

181.5 Bear right onto Route 7A south

182.8 End loop in downtown Lenox

The beginning of this loop goes through the busy town of Lee, then Route 20 loops back and forth across I-90 (Mass Pike) four times before reaching Bonny Rigg Corners. Route 8 north follows the west branch of the Westfield River and has lots of enjoyable twists and turns. If you aren't awake by now, these roads are eye-openers.

In the village of Dalton, just past Center Pond, the right turn is marked as Route 8A and Route 9. This is one of the major roads in the region (leading west to Pittsfield) and traffic can be heavy at times. Routes 8A and 9 divide in Windsor and in just a few miles, Route 9 becomes an enjoyable ride with plenty of swooping turns. The speed limit postings on this stretch of highway make no sense to me. Corners posted for 35 mph can be taken at a comfortable 80 mph without dragging pegs, but it does tend to bunch up traffic. Of course, blind corners and absurdly low posted speeds make this a place to watch for radar speed traps.

Route 112 is a pleasant but tame road all the way to Shelburne Falls. The center of his old mill town can be circumvented by way of a loop onto Route 2 and back onto the old Route 112 on the north edge of the village. The **Bridge of Flowers,** the old concrete railway bridge over the Deerfield River, is a unique garden spanning the river that attracts tens of thousands of visitors each year. The easiest way to reach it is to follow the bypass loop, but upon reaching Route 112 again, turn left. You can either turn right onto Cross Street (you'll see signs) or onto Main Street. On Main Street you'll see the Bridge of Flowers on your right as you cross the steel suspension bridge and can easily find parking on this side of the river. There are several restaurants in the downtown area, so, depending upon timing you might wish to enjoy an early lunch here, or wait until you reach Wilmington or Bennington.

The ride up Mt. Greylock proves the adage that it's the journey, not just the destination, that counts.

North of Shelburne Falls, Route 112 turns into one of the most popular motorcycling roads in New England. Since it connects with the famous Route 100 in Vermont, you'll have plenty of two-wheeled company on weekends. There are two steel suspension bridges with open-grate flooring that cross the East Branch North River on this route. The first is just north of Colrain and the second six-and-a-half miles farther; caution is advised for both of them. Route 112 passes by the North River Winery, then, four-tenths of a mile farther, junctions at Route 100 in the tiny village of Jacksonville.

The next five-and-a-half miles is a delight as the highway twists and turns through mostly forest as it climbs to Wilmington. If you are riding on a weekend be especially careful of traffic due to the large flea market located where Route 100 merges with Route 9 just east of Wilmington.

Wilmington is a popular village and with the local ski areas—Haystack, Mt. Snow, and even Stratton—offering summer events like world championship mountain biking competition and major concert series featuring top names, it can be a very busy place. **Dot's Restaurant,** adjacent to the small concrete bridge, is the place to stop for a late breakfast or gooood four-alarm chili (five alarms being the max). The chef has won a couple of Vermont state ribbons for the chili.

Mt. Greylock is popular for its three-state view at the top.

Your three-state view from the summit of Mt. Greylock

Route 9 still offers a few sections filled with exciting curves, especially just west of Wilmington, but since it is a major commercial highway, each year it seems that another corner gets straightened and there are miles of road where you can make very good time. Panoramic vistas and lower gear riding await you on the west side of the mountain range as you drop over 1,400 feet in elevation in the ten miles from Woodward to Bennington, including a three-mile stretch where signs recommend truck speed as 5 mph.

Bennington is the second-oldest settled township in Vermont, famous for its red clay pottery and Bennington College. The Sunoco gas station on Main Street is owned by **Hemmings Motor News** and you'll find some very interesting items for sale in its double bays; the musuem is located next door. The famous **Bennington Museum** is only four-tenths of a mile beyond the Sunoco station. A major collection of Grandma Moses paintings, Bennington pottery, and one of the major genealogical archives in the East are located here. Two-tenths of a mile farther is the right turn leading up to the Bennington Battle Monument. Although this battle, which was the turning point in the Revolutionary War, was actually fought in Hoosic, New York, the 306-foot tall monument was erected at the site of the storehouse that the British sought to capture. Most of the buildings in Old Bennington date to the end of the eighteenth century, and while George Washington never slept here, Thomas Jefferson and James Madison are among the notables who frequented the Walloomsac Inn (now a private residence). Behind the Old First Church, a well-marked path leads through the Old Burying Grounds to the gravesite of poet laureate Robert Frost.

Vermont Route 9 turns into New York Route 7, then Route 22 follows the western side of the Hoosic Range to Route 2. When the traffic isn't heavy on this road, the six-mile climb through the pass and the 3.8-mile twisting descent into Massachusetts is a delight.

Route 7 north leads to the intersection of Route 2 at the **Clark Art Institute** in beautiful Williamstown. The small downtown area has become completely encircled by the ever-expanding campus of Williams College. I suggest checking your fuel levels while on Route 2 and consider topping off your tank before continuing through the wilderness area of **Mt. Greylock.**

The Memorial Tower on the summit of Mt. Greylock, the highest mountain in Massachusetts.

Hemmings Sunoco is a pit stop to linger at. Check out the motorcycle and automotive memorabilia, books, and gifts. The museum is next door and a recommended tour.

After crossing the Hoosic River for the second time, you'll want to take your second right turn. This is a residential street leading to Notch Road. The terrible condition of Notch Road is notorious, but local residents prefer to leave it neglected to reduce traffic speed. Upon entering the reservation, the road narrows and resembles those in European alpine regions. It's first and second gear as you twist through the forest, climbing the shoulder of Mt. Greylock; beware of the deep trenches designed to channel water across the pavement! The top of the mountain at 3,491 feet is the highest peak in Massachusetts. Park and climb to the top of Memorial Tower for a spectacular 360-degree panoramic view. If you need to stretch your legs I suggest a stroll along a portion of the Appalachian Trail, which passes within a few yards of the tower. Despite the rough roads, this is one of the most popular motorcycle destinations in western Massachusetts, so expect plenty of company on any fine touring day, especially during the descent on Rockwell Road. (Note: don't bear right on the first Greylock Road you encounter; wait until Rockwell Road ends at the second intersection of the same name.)

The farther south you go on Route 7, the straighter and more commercial the road gets. Once you pass through the town of Pittsfield, after running along the shore of Pontoosuc Lake, it's a short run into the village of Lenox.

Trip 21 Southern Berkshire Loop

Distance *136 miles without side trips*

Highlights *Rural touring roads, scenic vistas, and places of historical interest*

The Route from Downtown Lenox

0.0 From the intersection of Main Street (Route 7A) and Walker Street (Route 183) in Lenox, proceed east on Walker Street

0.2 Bear left to stay on Route 183 east

1.0 Bear right onto Lee Road

1.2 Turn right onto Route 7 south and immediately bear left onto Route 20 east

12.0 At West Becket, turn right onto Route 8 south

38.3 At Winsted, Conn., turn right onto 44 west

This is the type of highway warning sign that raises the adrenalin level.

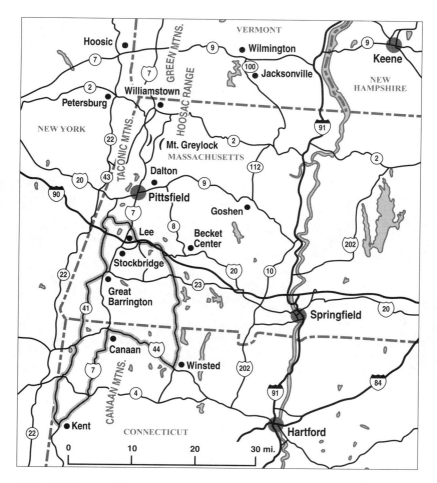

55.2 At Canaan, Conn., turn left onto Route 7 south

80.5 Just beyond Kent, Conn., turn right onto Route 341 west

83.3 As you cross into New York state, turn right onto Dutchess County Road (CR) 3

87.4 At South Amenia, turn right onto Dutchess County Road (CR) 2

89.9 At Amenia Union, turn right onto Route 41 north into Connecticut; pass through Great Barrington

130.6 After passing by the Mass. Turnpike (I-90, exit 1), turn right onto Lenox Road

134.2 Bear left onto Route 183

135.7 End at the junction of Routes 7A and 183 at Main Street in Lenox

The views from the observation deck of Memorial Tower on top of Mt. Greylock provide a spectacular 360-degree view of northern Massachusetts.

This is a simple route dedicated to a ride through mostly rolling countryside. Route 20 is busy through downtown East Lee until passing under Interstate 90. Signs on Route 8 warn of NARROW ROAD and SHARP CORNERS NEXT 14 MILES, but it's actually a pretty tame stretch of highway and you'll have no trouble sightseeing as you ride. Past West Becket, the turn to **Jacob's Pillow Dance Festival,** one of the foremost dance theaters in the region, is clearly marked. The tickets are tough to get, so order ahead.

South of the village of Otis, there are numerous paved pulloffs, many with picnic tables, along the Farmington River. As Route 8 broadens, it passes through 50- to 75-foot road cuts. The large body of water created by a dam on your left just north of Winstead is the Colebrook Reservoir.

A side trip on Route 20 east to the **Hitchcock Museum**—200 yards off of Route 20 on River Road in Riverton—has an extensive collection of Shaker furniture. Retrace your path back to Route 20 in Winstead to avoid the vortex of Hartford, Conn.

Route 7 is the main highway in western Connecticut and offers panoramic views across spacious farmland to the Taconic Mountain Range in the west.

The spectacular 200-foot high Kent Falls, which is just a short hike from the parking area in the Kent Falls State Park; the **Sloane-Stanley Museum** in Kent Furnace; and the village of Kent are all great places to stop and take a break. Try **Stroble's Baking and Catering** on Main Street for a quick bite to eat or a real cup of Belgian coffee or chocolate at **Belgique** at the junction of Route 341. When I ordered an iced chocolate even the ice cubes were made of chocolate milk!

If you have the time and inclination, a side trip (17-mile roundtrip on Route 202 east to New Preston) to **Hopkins Vineyards** is worth it. The inn and restaurant high on a hillside reminded me of a little alpine village from my European travels. The wine is pretty good too. Aim for the swill bucket, not the gullet at the tasting bar! If you swallow the wine, make it your last stop of the day. If you've made it this far, a ride around Lake Waramung (Route 45 north just outside of New Preston) is a necessity. If time permits, continue on Route 202 east to the famous village of Litchfield (51-mile roundtrip from Kent), a showcase of Colonial and Colonial Revival-styled architecture.

Route 41 is made for a bike. One of my favorite reminders of the difference between bikers and "everybody else" came from the gas station attendant at the intersection in Kent. When I asked him what Route 41 was like, he replied, "Where ya goin?" When I replied "Lenox, Mass." he screwed up his face and scratched his head in one of those looks asking, "Hell, why do you want to go 41? It's 15 miles outtayaway!" I thanked him and proceeded to have one decidedly delightful outtayaway trip!

It takes a bit of careful maneuvering on poorly marked county roads to reach Route 41, but it's worth it. Route 41 meanders north past beautiful farms and through small villages with the Taconic Mountains providing a scenic backdrop to the west. Sharon, which was once an important crossroads, has immaculate Victorian homes lining the green, but each village strung along this route has its own charm. Route 41 continues through Massachusetts, but just north of Richmond you turn onto Lenox Road. Roads in western Massachusetts, and especially in western Connecticut, have notoriously poor sign postings. I found the sign for Lenox Road actually hidden under a blanket of lush vines!

Lenox Road is an extremely beautiful stretch of road that leads to Route 183 at Tanglewood. The rest of the way into downtown Lenox is a pleasant cooling-down for your engine on a hot summer day.

Trip 22 Central Berkshire Loop

Distance *158 miles without side trips.*

Highlights *The loop features some country roads, portions of which go through the mountains, but it is more about the various site options that are available. The Indian Motorcycle Museum and the National Basketball Hall of Fame in Springfield and two eclectic art museums are just a sample of the possibilities on this loop in the central Berkshires.*

The Route from Downtown Lenox

0.0 From the intersection of Main Street (Route 7A) and Walker Street (Route 183) in Lenox, proceed west on Walker Street

1.6 Bear right onto Richmond Mountain Road

5.2 Near West Stockbridge, turn right onto Route 41 north

The roads of the Berkshires are narrow and twisty. Although the posted speeds are low, these rural roads are as much fun in third gear as any you'll find in New England.

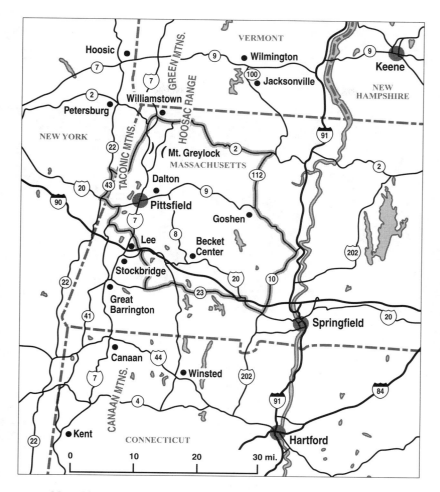

13.7 Near Pittsfield, turn left onto Route 20 west

18.9 Near New Lebanon, New York, turn right onto Route 22 north

19.1 Bear right to stay on Route 22 north

24.9 Turn right onto Route 43 north

37.4 At South Williamstown, Mass., turn left onto Route 7 north

41.6 At Williamstown, bear right onto Route 2 east

73.3 At Shelburne Falls, turn right onto Route 112 south

88.8 At Goshen, turn left onto Route 9 east

102.3 In Northampton, turn right onto Route 10 south

118.5 In Westfield, turn right onto Route 20 west

The Indian Motocycle Museum in West Springfield is worth the effort of a few miles of city riding. Many fantasies are generated with a visit to the museum.

124.2 At Woronoco, turn left onto Route 23 west

139.1 At Otis, turn right onto Routes 23 west/8 north

139.3 Bear left and proceed on Route 23 west

142.7 Near West Otis, turn right onto Tyringham Road

145.6 Near Tyringham, turn left onto Main Road

152.4 Near Lee, turn right onto Route 102 north

152.5 Turn left onto Route 20 west

156.5 Near Lenox, bear right onto Route 7 north and immediately bear left onto Lee Road

156.8 Bear left onto Route 183 west (Walker Street)

157.7 End of loop in downtown Lenox at the division of Routes 183 west/7A north

This time we head west on Route 183 to Richmond, bearing right at the **Tanglewood Music Center,** the summer home of the Boston Symphony Orchestra. During the summer schedule one can either sit on the lawn or buy seats for the performances. The park is lovely, so bring a picnic whether the orchestra is performing or not.

Richmond Mountain Road is a twisty and bumpy hill climb. Why do curves and bumps always go hand and glove? This turns into Lenox Road, which offers more curves and little traffic as it rolls up and down through the woods and past small farms. In Richmond, you take Route 41 north.

You'll discover the **Hancock Shaker Village** at the intersection of Routes 41 and 20. This is a restored settlement with 20 buildings on 1,000 acres and is one of the finer examples of the Shaker lifestyle.

The combination of Routes 20 west, 22 north, and 43 north are an enjoyable ride through and along the low mountains that form the boundary between Massachusetts and New York. They bring you to Route 7 north and into the beautiful Williamstown.

This is a Berkshire town with a blend of highbrow culture and a college environment. The original downtown area now appears to be the center of the campus rather than being the center of a village.

Stop at the **Sterling and Francine Clark Art Institute,** which houses the largest permanent collection of Renoirs in the United States. In addition to numerous works of the Old Masters and French Impressionists, the museum has an outstanding collection depicting the Old West through sculpture and paintings by Winslow Homer and Frederic Remington.

The story behind the Clark collection and museum is one of sibling rivalry. It seems the boys, Stephen and Robert Sterling, heirs to the Singer sewing machine fortune (their grandfather, Edward Clark, was Issac Singer's business partner) played a game of one-upmanship. In the end, Stephen donated his collection to the National Museum in Washington, D.C. Not to be outdone, Robert Sterling and his bride Francine built their own home to house their treasures, which in turn they transformed into the impressive museum—or mausoleum—bearing their name.

Route 2 follows what was once known as the **Mohawk Trail,** a major footpath used by the Indians of the Five Nations. The legend (which is mostly anecdotal) is that the Pocumtuck tribe blazed this trail across the mountains from Deerfield, Massachusetts to Troy, New York in order to invade the land of the Mohawks. The Dutch settlers in Albany negotiated a peace treaty to end the tribal war, but on the way to ratify this treaty, Shadeda, a Mohawk prince, was murdered on the trail. In retaliation, the Mohawks killed the entire Pocumtuck tribe in one day.

The first few miles of Route 2 west are along the commercial sprawl that lies between Williamstown and the old New England mill town of North Adams. Once past North Adams, the highway climbs into the Hoosic Mountain Range. Despite being a broad road that often has heavy car and truck traffic, it remains a delight for motorcyclists who enjoy cruising. The hairpin turn on the relatively gentle climb into the mountains is often photographically portrayed in guidebooks and articles on the Berkshires, but the fun portion of this road doesn't really begin until it descends between Clark and Todd mountains into the upper Deerfield Valley.

Route 112 south from Shelburne Falls takes you to Route 9 east. Both are enjoyable cruising roads with some nice corners and plenty of pavement. Route 9 goes to downtown Northampton and if you don't plan to stop and explore this upscale college town (Smith College is located here, with Amherst College and the University of Massachusetts just a few miles away in Amherst), which I highly recommend doing, you might consider stopping in Florence. The **Florence Diner** is a landmark and it's also the place to fortify yourself for the miles of congested city traffic that now face you.

Route 10 is almost all strip development as it heads south from Northampton through Easthampton, Southampton, and into Westfield. It's in Westfield that you'll encounter Route 20 and will have to make the choice as to whether to head west and escape the city as quickly as possible, or turn west and enter West Springfield on a side trip to the **Indian Motocycle Museum** (yep, that spelling is correct) and the **National Basketball Association Hall of Fame.**

From Westfield, take Route 20 east, crossing the Connecticut River and going under Interstate 91, and onto Route 291 east. It's 10.7 miles from Westfield to St. James Avenue (Exit 4 on I-291). Although it's marked as the exit for St. James Avenue, the ramp actually places you on Page Boulevard and you simply proceed straight, then turn right onto Hendee Street, the second street on your right. It's actually easy to find and the Indian Motocycle Museum certainly justifies the effort of having to hassle with city driving.

The National Basketball Association Hall of Fame is located on West Columbus Street at West Union, which places it between Interstate Highway 91 and the Connecticut River. From Route 20, you can go south on Route 5 (west side of the river) or I-91 (east side) to Route 147 (Memorial Bridge). Depending on which you take, you'll see signs for TO I-91 or TO ROUTE 5. West Columbus begins on the east side of the Memorial Bridge. Going by way of I-91, it's only 10.5 miles from Westfield.

Once out of Springfield, Route 23 becomes a special road: smooth with twisty turns, scenic hills, and deep forests. Twenty-eight miles west from Route 20, it enters into the town of Monterey, and you turn onto Tyringham Road. The eastern end of the Tyringham Road loop junctions at Route 23 east of Monterey. You can take a right onto the eastern end of Tyringham Road and continue to ride through the countryside, then proceed straight on Main Road, but if you wish to see The Gingerbread House (Tyringham Art

The Miss Florence Diner in Florence is a good place to stop and fortify yourself for the miles ahead.

Galleries), one of the most unusual structures in the region, continue into Monterey and make a right onto the *western* end of Tyringham Road.

The Gingerbread House, which looks like the witch's house in the fairy tale of *Hansel and Gretel,* was built as a design studio by the late Sir Henry Kitson (Sir Henry, the artist who sculpted the famous Minuteman Statue in Lexington, Mass. and who is represented in the National Gallery in Washington, D.C.). The roof of the building is made of shingles layered to simulate a thatched roof and carved to represent the contour of the Berkshires. You can see the texture sculpted to give the appearance of rolling hills and the burnished coloring of autumn. It houses an art gallery containing unique indoor and outdoor sculptures, mobiles, and ceramics.

Tyringham Road then continues through a residential area before encountering Main Road. Make sure to turn left and proceed west on Main Road or you'll find yourself looping back to Route 23. Main Road will take you to Route 20 in South Lee. In Lee, stop at **Joe's Diner,** a classic bit of 1950s Americana, for supper. While waiting for your meal you'll want to browse the pictures of famous patrons that adorn the walls. How many can you name without peeking at the autographs?

From Joe's Diner, it's either back to downtown Lenox or a shortcut onto Blantyre Road (a right turn just before the Cranwell Resort and Golf Course) and back to the campsite.

Places of Interest

CONNECTICUT

Kent

Belgique, the yellow carriage house at the intersection of Routes 7 and 341, Phone 860-927-3681. Open Thursday–Sunday Handmade Belgian chocolates, European pastries, coffee and hot chocolate. **Stroble's,** 14 N. Main Street, Route 7, Kent, 06757. Phone 860-927-4073. Pick up delightful pastries and sandwiches. Eat them on the tables outside or a beautiful turnoff somewhere along the way.

Kent Furnace

The Sloane-Stanley Museum, Route 7, Kent Furnace, at the old Kent Furnace site. Open Wednesday through Sunday, admission charged. A collection of early American tools collected by noted artist Eric Sloane (the land and buildings were donated by the Stanley Tool Company). The museum features a re-creation of Eric Sloane's studio and archives.

New Preston

Hopkins Vineyard and Inn, 25 Hopkins Road, New Preston, 06777. Phone 860-868-7954. www.hopkinsvineyard.com. Open every day for wine tasting and sales; dining serving Swiss and Austrian fare Tuesday through Sunday Reservations for the inn are a must. $$$

MASSACHUSETTS

Lanesborough

Bascom Lodge, Summit of Mt. Greylock. Phone 413-743-1591. One sitting, family style, 6:00 p.m. 100-mile views from the top. Reservations for dinner by noon. $$
Mt. Greylock State Reservation, Rockwell Road. Phone 413-499-4262. Thirty-five sites, primitive, highest point in Massachusetts. On the Appalachian Trail, picnics.

Lee

Joe's Diner, Route 20 and Main Street. Phone 413-243-9756. Open daily 6:00 a.m. to midnight. Famous 1950s luncheonette, good food, cheap daily specials. $

October Mountain State Forest, Woodland Road. Phone 413-243-1778. Fifty sites, well kept, close to loops and town. My base camp for the journey. Hot showers and campfires. It's the largest state forest in Massachusetts with 16,127 acres and hiking trails of all grades, including the Appalachian Trail and the scenic trail to Schermerhorn Gorge.

Lenox

Cherry's, 6 Franklin Street. No phone. Open daily 6:30 a.m. to 8:00 p.m. (Monday and Tuesday to 2:00 p.m.). Managed by local school kids, open mike Friday 'til midnight, daily lunch and dinner specials. $

Pittsfield

Dakota, Route 7. Phone 413-499-7900. Daily lunch and dinner. Fresh continental fare. Largest salad bar I know. Treat yourself. $$$

Shelburne Falls

Marty's Riverside Cafe, 4 State Street. Phone 413-625-2570. Open year-round, 11:00 a.m. to 9:00 p.m., closed Mondays. Funky natural food on the river, specials daily. $$

Springfield

Indian Motocycle Museum, 33 Hendee Street. Phone 413-737-2624. Open March to November, 10:00 a.m. to 5:00 p.m., and December to February, 1:00 to 5:00 p.m. Admission $3. It's a pilgrimage!

National Basketball Hall of Fame, 1150 West Columbus Avenue. Phone 413-781-6500. Open year-round 9:00 a.m. to 5:00 p.m., July and August until 6:00 p.m. Admission $6. If you are a fan, this is a behind-the-back slam dunk.

Williamstown

Sterling and Francine Clark Art Museum, 225 South Street. Phone 413-458-9545. Open year-round, Tuesday to Sunday 10:00 a.m. to 5:00 p.m. Culture and art, free of charge.

VERMONT

Wilmington

Dot's Restaurant, Route 9. Phone 802-464-7284. Open daily 5:30 a.m. to 3:00 p.m. Diner and luncheonette. Cajun omelets, four-star chili, homemade muffins. $

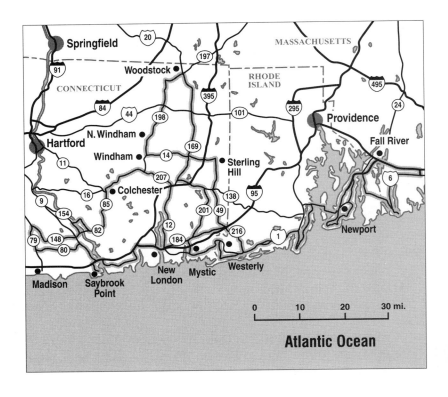

Sightseeing the Southern Coast

The southern coast of New England—Connecticut, Rhode Island, and Massachusetts—was the whaling and fishing capital of the United States in the mid-1800s. Of the 739 whaling ships that roamed the world at that time, over 400 of them called home New Bedford or Fairhaven, Massachusetts. Even today, New Bedford has the largest fishing fleet in the country, more than 300 ships. If you want some idea of why the ocean is so important here, consider this: although Rhode Island, the smallest state in the U.S., is only 45 miles across, it has more than 400 miles of shoreline.

It is because of this geography that the loops on this journey appear short and the views from the steed are to the horizon. This journey is scenic, historic, and a real "beach," where riders can take the sun, explore naval history, go whale watching, or all three. I integrated curving and cresting interior roads into the journey for variety in scenery and ride mix. Some are through lush farmland with traditional stone walls separating crops from animals. Others lead to major attractions like the popular gaming casinos of the Mashantucket Pequot Tribal Nation or the Essex Steam Train and Riverboat rides that recreate life on the river and the rails.

Home base for this "SeaFairing" journey is **Burlingame State Park** off Route 1, between Westerly and Charlestown, Rhode Island, a comfortable enclave with lovely tall pines and its own pond for swimming and fishing, yet only minutes from the sea. Fisherman's Memorial State Park (reservations required) is an alternative off Route 108 between Narragansett and Point Judith, Rhode Island.

The Bay Loop crosses the border between Rhode Island and Massachusetts a number of times, and the Inland Loop comes close to crossing the Massachusetts border from Connecticut. A word of caution: as of this writing, there is no helmet law in Rhode Island for adults age 21 and over or Connecticut for adults age 18 and over, but Massachusetts enforces the requirement strictly for all riders.

Trip 23   Bay Loop

Distance   *174 miles*

Highlights   *Hundreds of miles of scenic coastline lead to great beaches, famous fishing ports, museums at every turn, and fabulous Newport, home of mansions, 50-foot yachts, and one of the country's oldest outdoor jazz festivals. Your pace will be slow—this is a popular area especially in summer—and besides, you'll want to stop and savor the sea air, fresh fish, and your step back into history.*

The Route from Burlingame State Park

0 mi   Exit Burlingame State Park on the access road and turn left on R.I. Route 1 north

14.1   Exit "Narragansett/Point Judith" and turn right on Route 108 south to Point Judith

18.3   Turn left on Route 108 north to Ocean Road, Narragansett

Seamen's Bethel in New Bedford was an inspiration for Herman Melville and his classic Moby Dick.

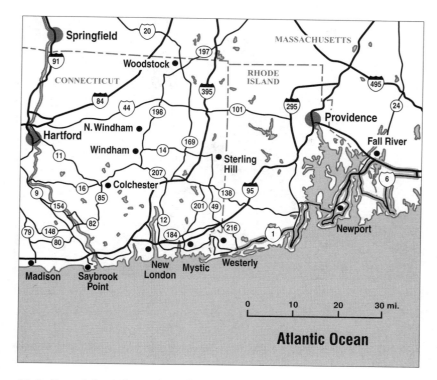

23.2 Bear right as Ocean Road merges with Route 1A north at Narragansett

30.5 Turn *left* onto entrance ramp to Route 138 east to cross bridges at Newport

37.5 Take first exit after Newport Bridge at SCENIC NEWPORT sign

37.6 Bear right onto Thames Street when the sign for Memorial Boulevard and Route 138 indicates a left

40.4 Turn left onto Ocean Drive until it connects with Bellevue Ave at Bailey's Beach

41.2 Turn left onto Bellevue Avenue

43.1 Turn right onto Memorial Boulevard

44.5 Bear left onto Route 138A north which merges with Route 138 north/138 east (signs inconsistent)

58.5 Bear left on Route 24 north

62.5 Exit NORTH TIVERTON and turn left onto Route 138 north

68.8 Exit right at DAVOL STREET and double-back on water side to Battleship Cove

The Widow's Watch on this typical shore home lets you see over the high dunes and out to sea.

69.8 Exit Battleship Cove and turn left onto Route 138 north and right onto I-195 east

82.9 Take Exit 15 DOWNTOWN NEW BEDFORD onto Route 18 south and follow brown signs to parking for the Whaling Museum at Elm Street Garage

84.4 Exit right from garage on Elm Street for 2 ½ blocks, turn right on Pleasant Street to rotary and exit west on Mill Street which is Route 6 west

90.7 Turn left on Route 177 west

92.6 Turn left on Route 88 south to Horseneck Beach

101.2 Turn left at water and follow shore road to South Westport

108.9 Turn left on Hixbridge Road, cross Route 88, right at T, left at Westport Lobster Co. to Adamsville

113.6 Turn right onto Route 179 west

117.1 Turn right onto Route 77 north

124.6 Turn left onto Route 24 south/138 south which becomes Route 114 south

129.1 Continue on Route 114 south which becomes Route 138 west

145.8 Exit right from Route 138 west after bridge onto Route 1A south

157.0 At light at Narragansett, turn right on Narragansett Ave to Route 1 south

158.4 Turn left onto Route 1 south

174.2 Exit BURLINGAME STATE PARK CAMPING to home base.

The Bay Loop can easily take two to three days depending on how much beach, culture, and sightseeing you want to do. This is an extensive trip, although the mileage is short. The Bay Loop passes the most beautiful beaches and breathtaking shoreline in New England. Many of the oldest shipping ports in the nation are along the way.

From the late 1800s to the mid-1900s, some of the wealthiest people in the world chose Newport and its surroundings to live in. They built mansions on the cliffs above the sea that rival the palaces of European royalty, and many are open to tour and enjoy. Narragansett Bay is still the summer playground for the rich, but more modest folk can play here, too. And you will want to get off the bike and explore the many unique attractions this area has to offer. Water sports abound and this may be the perfect time to take a whale watch cruise or a hike on the famous Cliff Walk. Parking is plentiful and on average, safe.

Hammersmith Farm in Newport, Rhode Island, was JFK's summer White House. Scenes from The Great Gatsby *were filmed here.*

*New Bedford's
Historic District
has cobblestone
streets and
gorgeous
architecture.*

The first things you notice while riding on Route 1 east and north from home base (the highway department is inconsistent in their signage) are the exit signs on the way to Narragansett. Every one of the signs names a beach: Charlestown Beach Road, Moonstruck Beach Road, Matunuck Beach Road, and just for variety, a sign for the Theater by the Sea. All within ten miles of where you first got on the road.

Route 108 south, off of Route 1, is a four-lane undivided highway. If you have the time and decide to go to **Block Island,** take Galilee Road just beyond Fisherman's Memorial State Park. This takes you into Galilee, where the Block Island Ferry docks. Just 12 miles off the coast and called by some "one of the last great places on earth," it's very much worth the brief ride. There is a bustling harbor with shops and beautifully restored Victorian-era inns and houses, a bird sanctuary, and acres of beautiful pristine open space

This is the Casino Arch on Ocean Avenue at Narragansett. If you want a casino see the "Above and Below Loop."

to enjoy. You can take your motorcycle on the ferry if you want, but you may prefer a break from the saddle. Bicycles are for rent on the island and the walking is superb.

Continuing south on Route 108, you arrive at **Point Judith Light.** The lighthouse itself is a mile down the road to the right after you see the water and is now a Coast Guard station not accessible to the public. The last German U-Boat sunk in World War II was two miles off this point.

When you retrace your steps from the lighthouse, continue straight on Ocean Road rather than turning left onto Route 108. Over the next eight miles of winding road hugging the sea, you'll pass eight beaches and some wonderful early summer houses. Scarborough State Beach is a surfing beach, so there's plenty of action at the sea and on the shore for us buoys and gulls who are young or young at heart.

Farther up the road is the town of Narragansett and its even more active beaches. If you're interested, check to see if they still give free surfing lessons on Wednesdays at noon. But watch the conditions. The last time I was through, a Nor'easter was on its way and the surf was blowing over the seawall leaving the road covered in a foot of foam. For me, the best features of Narragansett town beach are the so-close-at-hand establishments serving cold refreshments. **The Coast Guard Restaurant** has a nice observation deck for the scenery.

Want lunch with a view? Try the Coast Guard Restaurant on Ocean Road.

Narragansett was (and is) an elegant summer resort. In the late 1800s, rich Newporters would ferry across the bay to partake of the entertainment offered by the Narragansett Casino, a country club by today's definition. A fire destroyed the casino in 1900. All that's left is the dramatic stone arch and towers over Ocean Road.

Route 1A north intersects with Route 138 about eight miles up. Follow signs east to Newport and Jamestown Bridge. The Jamestown Bridge and the Newport Bridge on the other side of Conanicut Island offer spectacular views of Narragansett Bay.

(See Side Trip to Conanicut Island)

Back on Route 138 east, cross the Newport Bridge ($2 toll) from Jamestown to Newport. Keep one eye on the bridge traffic, but check out the harbor and the yachts as you cross. Welcome to the land of the rich and the tourists! You will have to put up with traffic in the town of Newport as it is a popular destination resort, especially in the warm months.

Just as you enter the wharf area, you'll spot the **Newport Transportation and Visitors Center** on your right, an invaluable resource for accommodations, sightseeing, and events if you plan to stay a day or two. Downtown hotels, inns, and B&Bs are pricey but if you want to treat yourself, this may be the time to splurge. The **Newport Harbor Hotel and Marina** will cost you close to $200 per night but the rooms are first class and overlook the boats in the harbor. The hotel even provides binoculars on your window sill for a close-up look.

If you're watching your budget but still want to stay overnight, head for one of the more modest motels on the outskirts of town, or ask for a recommendation in your price range at the Visitors Center. There's something for every pocketbook here.

Fine eating places abound but you might want to try the **Red Parrot Restaurant** on the corner of Thames Street and Memorial Boulevard and a short

➡ Side Trip to Conanicut Island

The Jamestown Bridge deposits you onto Conanicut Island, as serene as its more famous neighbor, Newport, is sophisticated. If you stay straight on East Shore Road, rather than following Route 138, you'll arrive in the village of Jamestown. Park in the lot at the harbor and have a cup of award-winning coffee and pastry at **East Ferry Market & Deli** out on the patio overlooking the bay.

Facing the water from your patio perch, take the road in front of you to the right, following the shoreline to Fort Wetherill State Park, once a shore artillery battery. Picnic tables and the usual day-tripper facilities are available from Memorial Day to Labor Day. The park itself remains open all year. This is a favorite spot among scuba divers.

Exiting the park, take your first paved left, Hamilton St, which is flanked by some pretty spectacular new homes. At the next intersection, go straight ahead; a small town beach will be on your left. Go across the isthmus. On the right, just at the end of the isthmus, is the entrance to Fort Getty State Park, a seaside campground sitting on a small knoll, with a magnificent view, overlooking the mouth of Narragansett Bay. Although it is usually full during camping season, it's worth a drive through.

Bear left onto Beaver Tail Road just after the Fort Getty entrance to get to **Beavertail Lighthouse State Park.** The lighthouse is the third oldest in the country, built in 1749 after the Boston Light (1716) and the Brant Point Light on Nantucket (1746). The museum inside commemorates the lighthouses of Rhode Island and their keepers.

You can either retrace your trip back to Route 138 or take Southwest Avenue to North Main Street to the bridge. The latter route lets you check out the **Jamestown Windmill,** which is right beside the road just before you reach Route 138. It's interesting to see anytime but you can learn how it works when the windmill itself is open to visitors on Saturdays and Sundays, 1–4 p.m., from mid-June to mid-September. ■

walk from The Newport Harbor Hotel and Marina. They advertise "hot" desserts and "cool" jazz, along with fresh seafood, creative pasta, and unique appetizers. Get a window seat and you can check out the passing sidewalk scene, which is always pretty colorful on busy Thames Street For breakfast, the locals go to the **Franklin Spa,** a short walk up the hill on Spring Street for grease and gab.

To get to the famous **Ten Mile Drive,** take a right onto Wellington Avenue as you circumnavigate the harbor. This is a spectacular scenic ride along the coast, past all the humble abodes of the more fortunate. Two outstanding examples are the Hammersmith Farm and the Inn at Castle Hill.

The Hammersmith Farm, a.k.a. "the Summer White House," was Jackie Kennedy Onassis' mother's (Mrs. Hugh Auchincloss) summer home. Jackie had her debut and her wedding reception with JFK here. The fifty acres of farmland by the sea make up the only working farm in Newport. Scenes from *The Great Gatsby,* with Robert Redford, were filmed here.

The **Inn at Castle Hill** just down the road (watch for signs since you can't see it from the road) offers a panoramic view of the bay. Watch the great ships entering and leaving the harbor while you sit on the patio enjoying something cold to drink, then walk to the cliff's edge to see Castle Hill Light.

Back on the Ten Mile Drive, you will shadow the ocean's edge until you reach Bellevue Avenue. This is where the **Great Mansions of Newport**

Point Judith Light and Coast Guard station.

It's hard to miss George's Family Restaurant in Fall River, Massachusetts, and his great homemade root beer.

were (Vander)built in pre-income-tax America. You can tour them (it takes a good day or two to do all ten properties that are now open to the public). If your schedule is tight, choose just one, and make it **The Breakers,** Cornelius Vanderbilt II's opulent 70-room Italian Renaissance palace where balconies and terraces overlook a spectacular view of the Atlantic Ocean. The furnishings, most made expressly for the house, are all original. The tour takes about an hour and tickets ($15 for adults) can be purchased at the gatehouse.

If you are just passing through, take a minute to drive into a few of the entrances (I hesitate to call them driveways) and get a feel for the grandeur of these elegant "summer homes." It's amazing to think that some of them were used by their owners for only a few weeks of the year. Others like the Vanderbilt family stayed all summer with Cornelius commuting on weekends by steamer from New York City. Imagine your arrival as a guest, then play it out: at the Astor's Beechwood Mansion, the Beechwood Theatrical Group welcomes your arrival as if you were one of the original "Newport 400" arriving for the season in the 1890s.

Once your "coming out" party is over, rejoin Memorial Boulevard, merge with Route 138 north, pass through Tiverton, R.I., and head straight for Fall River, Mass. on Route 24 north. Just after the Rhode Island border, on Route 138 in Massachusetts and on the left, is the un-miss-able **George's Root Beer,** a white and blue building with bright yellow sandwich boards out front

Battleship Cove in Fall River Heritage State Park is home to the world's largest collection of historic battleships.

advertising $2–$4 dinners. George makes his own root beer, and it is delicious. If it's too early for a cold one, three blocks farther on is the **Sip and Dip Donut Drive Thru,** another not-to-be-missed "original," with homemade donuts and the owner's daughter-in-law, Lucy, at the window. They open at 4:30 a.m. and don't close until 11:00 p.m. I can't guarantee that Lucy works 24/7, although she's the type who might!

Follow the signs to **Battleship Cove,** "the world's largest collection of historic naval ships," and Fall River Heritage State Park. You will see the battleships in the cove to your left just after Route 138 north goes under I-195. Route 138 north is elevated at this point so it's quite a view. Exit right at Davol Street and double back on the water side to park for free and walk around the cove to the ships. The USS Massachusetts, affectionately called "Big Mamie," by her crew, is over 200 yards long. You can tour the entire ship, climb inside the turrets, and aim the anti-aircraft guns on the main deck. You can also patrol a PT boat, a destroyer, a submarine, and the Hiddensee, the only Russian missile corvette on display in the world.

The **Marine Museum** down the street has a excellent exhibition focused on the Titanic, including a video of her rediscovery and a 28-foot replica. There's also a Railroad Museum and the magnificent old wooden carousel from the Lincoln Amusement Park to explore, so leave a good part of the day free to do it all. The **Waterstreet Cafe** is just across the street and a good choice for a light snack or a full meal.

Before exiting **Fall River Heritage State Park,** check out the little museum there too. It has a small theatre and rotating exhibits depicting the rich ethnic history of the people who came to Fall River and made it their home. From the 1840s to the 1920s, waves of immigrants predominantly from England, Ireland, Canada, Portugal, and Poland came to work in the textile mills and the shipping yards. The city was believed to have the largest percentage of foreign-born people of any major American population center, and their cultural pride still exists today.

Follow signs to Interstate Route 195 and go east to Exit 15, DOWNTOWN NEW BEDFORD, and Route 18 south. Watch for the brown whale (picture) signs to the NEW BEDFORD WHALING NATIONAL HISTORIC PARK, which will direct you to exit onto Elm Street. Because New Bedford still has cobblestone streets in the Historic District, which does nothing for traction, especially if wet, I recommend you park in the Elm Street garage ($3–$4) and walk the three blocks to the museum itself.

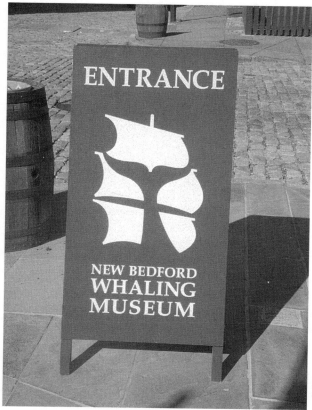

At the New Bedford Whaling Museum you'll have a chance to see the big ones that didn't get away.

It looks like you can do pretty much whatever you want between November and March at the Westport Town Beach.

The **New Bedford Whaling Museum** is devoted to American whaling, with a multi-media approach to this period of history. There are paintings, artifacts, harpoons, whale skeletons, murals, and an 85-foot exact half-scale model built in 1916 of the whaling ship *Lagoda.* You can shiver your own timbers on board—it's as though you climbed into one of those "ship in the bottle" models!

On my last trip through, the theater was showing a fascinating movie on the rich history of the area called *The City That Lit the World,* which among other things included a reenactment of a whaling expedition. For the real thing, check out the TV monitor near the *Lagoda* replica for another film made in 1922 in New Bedford on board an actual whaling ship. An actor portrays Charles W. Morgan, the boat's owner and namesake of the Charles W. Morgan Whaleship moored in Mystic Seaport, Conn., and built in New Bedford.

Across the street is the **Seamen's Bethel.** Built in 1832, it provided inspiration for Herman Melville's whaling classic, *Moby Dick.* Melville's sister, whom he came to visit often, lived in New Bedford. The cenotaphs (memorial stones on the walls) commemorate sailors who sailed out of New Bedford and never returned. The plaque at the entrance reads from the novel, "In the same New Bedford there stands a whalesman's chapel and few are the moody fishermen shortly bound for the Indian or Pacific Oceans who failed to make a Sunday visit to this spot."

Time to head for home, so pick up Route 6 west, which is commercial and congested but a means to an end, and follow it to Route 177 west.

Stay on Route 177 if you want to shorten the loop, or shoot down Route 88 (watch your speed on this 55 mph runway) for more beaches and more coast to explore. **Horseneck Beach** is a Massachusetts state park with day parking, camping, and a whole bunch of diverse people. During the good weather, the RVs are lined up right at the water's edge and it's easy to see why the spot is so popular, but as the "no" sign on the Westport Town Beach section says, there's to be "no horse play" from April 1st to November 1st. In the winter, I guess you can do what you want.

After you've had your fill of sea air, work your way back up on the country lanes to Tiverton and the crossing to the Newport peninsula and then onto the bridges into Rhode Island proper.

No matter which option you choose however, watch for Brickley's Homemade Ice Cream on the left of Route 1A south (about four miles after you exit Route 138 west at the end of the Jamestown Bridge) and just past the idyllic Casey Farm which will be on your right. As I often find with places like this, small is large and large is humongous and unliftable, so watch what you order, but the cones are scrumptious and they make the ice cream right in the back.

At the light at Narragansett, cut over to Route 1 and head for your little home among the pines at **Bulingame State Park Camping Area.**

Small is Large and Large is HUMONGOUS at Brickley's where they make the ice cream in back, so you can add it to your front.

Trip 24 Inland Loop

Distance *154 miles without side trips*

Highlights *Miles of perfectly banked two-lane country back roads will have you believing that you and the steed really are one. Lean to the left, lean to the right, up and over a small whoop-de-do, down a tree-canopied lane, the traffic is light and there's not a McDonald's in sight. Top off the tank before you start. At the end of a beautiful riding day, spend an hour or two at Mystic Seaport and then enjoy a coastal sunset from Stonington Light, Watch Hill, or the beaches at Misquamicut.*

Climb to the top of the light at Stonington's Old Lighthouse Museum for a dramatic 360 degree view of the ocean.

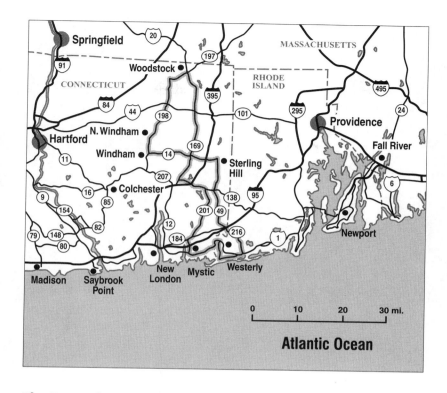

The Route from Burlingame State Park

0 mi Turn right out of Burlingame State Park to Route 216 north

1.3 Turn right onto Route 216 north

12.4 At North Stonington, bear right onto Route 49 north

30.0 At Sterling Hill, turn left onto Route 14A

37.1 At Canterbury, turn right onto Route 169 north

58.7 At , turn left onto Route 197 west

64.1 Turn left onto Route 198 south

80.2 Turn right onto Route 6 west

82.0 At North Windham, turn left onto Route 203 south

85.6 At Windham, take two lefts onto Route 14 east

95.8 At Canterbury, turn right onto Route 169 south

103.0 Turn left on Route 138 east

111.1 Turn right onto Route 201 south

125.4 Continue straight as Route 201 south merges with Route 184 west

Roseland, a Gothic among the Victorians, across from Woodstock Green, Connecticut

126.8 At Old Mystic, turn left onto Route 27 south

130.0 At Mystic, turn left onto Route 1 east

137.8 At Westerly, Rhode Island, turn right onto Route 1A

141.5 Bear right on Watch Hill Road, round the point, and follow coastal road east

149.8 Rejoin Route 1A east

150.6 Bear right onto Route 1

153.3 Turn left onto access road for Burlingame State Park Camping

153.9 Arrive at campground

After all the tight quarters and museums of the Bay Loop, it's time to stretch our steeds a bit. The first 130 miles of this loop are scenic riding at its best with some twists and room to wail (or should I say whale?). Take a right out of the campground onto a narrow two-lane twisty with some sand patches on the curves (reminds me of an old beach road) so don't open it up too much. Route 216 is like a country lane with pine tree stands; more throttle, please. Route 49 opens up even more, with forest on one side and rolling farmland on the other. Route 14A tightens with ascending and descending roads, another vote for east/west roads. Route 169 straightens and opens. This is a day to feel the road and test your skills. There are no major attractions to distract you, just good riding through some very beautiful countryside.

As you pass through, you'll note that many of the towns along this loop have statues to commemorate their American Revolution war heroes. In Brooklyn, Conn. stands the imposing statue of General Israel Putnam, Esq. It was "Old Put" who, at the Battle of Bunker Hill, issued the command "Don't fire until you see the whites of their eyes!" Other towns honor their American Revolution heritage with historical plaques.

At Pomfret, you'll definitely want to stop at the **Vanilla Bean Café** on the northwest corner of the Route 244 intersection. Barry and Brian Jessurun, who own the place, are both motorcyclists and you'll often see lots of bikes parked in front by the outdoor patio. Voted "Top Stop" four years in a row by the Worcester, Mass. Harley-Davidson Owners Group, the food is truly delicious and the company can't be beat. Try their homemade soups, award-winning chili, or a decadent dessert to die for.

Route 197 west gets you going again (if you can stand that is, after eating at the Bean) with some tight curves. But first you might want to make a short side trip to see popular **Thompson Speedway** just to the east on Route 200 if you're into sports car racing.

Owned by a motorcycling family, The Vanilla Bean Cafe is popular with the local riders for its award-winning chili and decadent desserts.

Route 198 is a remote road, so remote that as I was tooling along, I came across a fox just lying on the asphalt, warming in the sun. If it's lunchtime and you didn't already blow your appetite at the Bean, stop at the **Stoggy Hollow Restaurant and General Store** on the right about three miles down. Named for the wooden pegs used to make leather shoes at the now defunct Woodstock Shoe Factory, Stoggy Hollow is another favorite of the local bikers who often can be found on the open deck watching the action on the road below. If a picnic appeals, this is also a good place to grab a delicious deli sandwich and some homemade bakery items. Perfect spots by the river are around every corner on this scenic back road.

Don't miss the magnificent equestrian statue of General Putnam in Brooklyn, Connecticut. He issued the famous command, "Don't fire until you see the whites of their eyes," at the Battle of Bunker Hill.

Route 14 winds east to Route 169 and more scenic farmlands. This is also good wine country but easy on the sampling. There's still much to see and do ahead. Route 201 south is a pretty country lane following the contours of the land and you'll enjoy scraping pegs as you cap the riding day.

OK, you've finished your exercise and it's back to civilization and history, i.e., Mystic Seaport.

This is the largest maritime museum in the United States. Located on 17 acres along the Mystic River, the museum is home to such ships as the Charles W. Morgan, the last wooden whaling bark of a fleet that numbered over 700 in the mid-1800s. A full working portrayal of sea and seaport life in the 1800s is here to explore: a ship chandlery, rigging loft, cooperage (cask and barrel making), sailor's tavern, and restoration shop, among other exhibits. **Mystic Seaport** is a popular place, so be prepared for the crowds in summer. A visit can easily take a full day, depending on your fascination factor. Do not budget less than a half-day to justify the $17 admission fee.

Another popular attraction in the area is the **Mystic Aquarium,** "where there's always something new, so dive in." Open year round, it's a good spot to spend a rainy day playing with the interactive displays, multi-media exhibits, and other hands-on experiences.

(See Side Trip to Stonington)

The open deck at the Stoggy Hollow Restaurant and General Store is the perfect spot for a picnic and view of the two-wheel goings-on the road below.

Mystic Seaport is the largest maritime museum in the United States. You can easily spend a half day here.

Rejoin Route 1A at the end of the strip and follow it. Once you're over the border into Rhode Island, head for Watch Hill. This village is a miniature Newport with huge mansions overlooking the sea. The town also boasts the world's oldest carousel, but it's for little kids only. Don't worry though, **Misquamicut,** an original honky-tonk beach town, has all the big-kid rides. Sporting Ferris wheels, bumper cars and go-karts, water slides, and New York-style hot dogs (it's like a chili dog without the flame), Misquamicut has beach bars, deck bars, rock 'n' roll bars, discos, and general cruising at night. It's a fun place to be, and about 10 minutes from the campground. If you're imbibing, stay at one of the many motels on the strip.

Continue on Route 1 east to close the loop. If you are still hungry or thirsty, grab a freshly made wrap and a cool one at **Michael's Mart and Garage** on the right just past the Route 216 intersection and enjoy it under the stars at home base.

There's always something new at the Mystic Aquarium, so hop in!

➡ Side Trip to Stonington

Bear right onto Route 1A for a visit to the charming and historic village of Stonington. Continue straight through town to the point and the **Old Light House Museum.** From the parking lot, you'll have a dramatic 360-degree view of the ocean. The view is even better from the top of the lighthouse and you are encouraged to climb the ancient granite steps to see for yourself. The museum itself is a jewel and you'll want to save some time to visit the exhibits. The whale bone rib and a perfectly preserved Civil War drum caught my eye, but there's much of interest. It makes you think that the families of Stonington have been there for generations and each has contributed its best treasures to the little granite lighthouse. As you exit town, note Mystic Pizza I at 56 West Main Street.., the focus and setting for the 1988 hit movie that starred Julia Roberts.   ■

Trip 25 Above and Below Loop

Distance *198 miles*

Highlights *A combination of country roads, river roads, shoreline drives, interesting attractions and a little bit of traffic come together for a nice ride that's never the same and will keep you interested all day long. Spend the morning touring a nuclear sub, have lunch and hopefully luck at a casino, and the afternoon looking at steam engines, river boats, and a castle.*

The Route from Burlingame State Park

0 mi Exit right out of Burlingame State Park to Route 216 north

1.3 Turn right onto Route 216 north

9.9 Turn left onto Route 184 west

Beautiful stone walls are everywhere and this is an excellent example of one built to last.

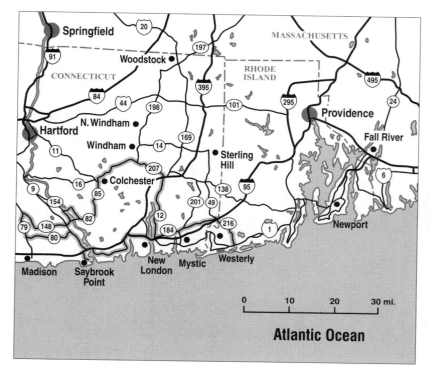

25.2 Turn right onto Route 12 north

26.8 Turn left onto Crystal Lake Road

27.2 Arrive at the USS Nautilus outside U.S. submarine base

27.6 At the intersection of Crystal Lake Road and Route 12, turn left onto Route 12 north

35.1 Turn right onto 2A east to visit Foxwoods Casino

37.7 Turn right onto Route 2 east

41.9 Enter access road to Foxwoods Casino; after your visit, return to this point and turn left onto Route 2 west

48.9 In Norwich, turn right onto Route 12 north

56.9 At Jewett City, turn left onto Route 138 west

62.7 Turn left onto Route 97 south

62.8 At Baltic, pick up Route 207 west

74.3 Turn left onto Route 16 south

79.4 At Colchester, turn left onto Route 85 south

Crossing the Connecticut River at Hadlyme, the Haddam Swing Bridge offers a most unique approach to river navigation.

80.6 Turn right onto Lake Hayward Road (first right after Route 2 underpass)

81.5 Turn left onto Lake Shore Road

84.7 Take right onto Haywardville Road

86.4 Turn left onto Hopyard Road, toward Devil's Hopyard State Park

90.6 Turn right onto Route 82 west

94.1 At intersection, follow Route 148 west to Gillette's Castle

95.7 At Gillette's Castle, reverse direction and return on Route 148 east

97.2 At junction, turn left onto Route 82 west

103.4 Across river at Tylerville, turn left onto Route 154 south

106.5 Turn right onto Route 148 west

120.6 Turn left onto Route 79 south

126.4 At North Madison, turn left onto Route 80 east (around traffic circle)

136.5 Continue straight on unmarked road toward Ivoryton and Centerbrook

138.4 At stop in Ivoryton, bear left toward OLD SAYBROOK/WESTBROOK

139.8 Continue straight through Centerbrook

140.5 Turn right onto Route 154 south and proceed to Saybrook Point

147.0 At Saybrook Point, retrace your path

149.2 Turn right onto Route 1 north

149.6 Turn right onto Route 95 east to cross the river

151.8 Take Exit 70 from Route 95 east onto Route 156 east

162.4 At Niantic, turn left onto Route 161 north

165.3 Turn right onto Route 95 east to Groton

173.2 Turn right onto Route 184 east at Groton

188.8 Turn right onto Route 216 south

197.5 Turn left into Burlingame State Park and home base

Goodspeed Opera House is a fully restored Victorian theatre built in 1876. You can catch a backstage tour if you're a behind-the-scenes person.

Route 184 offers a country road alternative to both Interstate 95 and Route 1, a fact you can use for the previous loops. The **USS Nautilus and Submarine Force Museum** is definitely worth the visit. It serves as the official repository for the records and history of the United States Submarine Force, from its beginnings at the turn of the century to the modern Navy. The museum should take about one hour to tour and the *Nautilus* about 30 minutes. Outside the museum are actual midget submarines used in early exploration during World War I and World War II by the German, Japanese, and Italian navies. As you enter the museum, an 11-foot model of Captain Nemo's *Nautilus* faces you. The museum is geared for sound, sight, and touch. A recreated submarine attack center stirs the imagination when you hear the sounds of battle from "down below." You can also use real periscopes to see submarines head up the river outside the building to the sub pens in Groton, though I didn't see any on my visit.

The museum has two mini-theaters with five-minute continuous loop films. Upstairs is a 50-foot cutaway replica of the *USS Gato* and a film of actual World War II battle scenes, with U.S. subs attacking and sinking a fleet of Japanese surface ships. Then the incongruity hit me: the film is shown on a Hitachi television. Hmmmmm!

The Nautilus, America's first nuclear submarine, makes for an exciting tour. Shut the screen door please!

Now it's time for the real thing. Climbing aboard the *USS Nautilus, SSN 571,* standing on her deck, and preparing to go below, I anticipated coming face to face with what until now had been only a legend to me. The guards handed me a telephone-shaped device that provided a self-paced tour, and I descended into the world's first nuclear sub. Launched on January 21, 1954 by Mamie Eisenhower, the *USS Nautilus* was the first ship to cross the geographic North Pole, 90 degrees north! It is hard to believe that over a hundred men lived in such tight quarters. At the time, these were spacious. The museum is free.

After you've had your fill of subs (hold the baloney), return to Route 12 and head north seven miles to Connecticut's newest attractions, the casinos. While you may not have time to try your luck, **Foxwoods Resort and Casino** is a sight one should behold, with its towers gleaming high above the treetops and its 6,500 slot machines and 350 gaming tables going full tilt night and day. The resort includes three hotels with over 1,400 luxurious rooms and deluxe suites, a spa, 24 restaurants and eateries, star-studded entertainment, and a shopping concourse to rival Rodeo Drive. The **Mohegan Sun** with its Casinos of the Sky and Earth on the western side of the river is a slightly smaller version of Foxwoods. Both are operated by the Mashantucket Pequot Tribal Nation on their reservation land. Nestled in the woods less than a mile from Foxwoods is the **Mashantucket Pequot Museum and Research Center** with feature films, videos, interactive programs, crafts, multi-sensory dioramas, and exhibits depicting the culture and heritage of Native American life. Well worth a visit.

Back on Route 12 north, you will meander along the Thames River to its headwaters, past Norwich, Connecticut, an interesting old mill town, and to I-395, where you pick up Route 138 west. Routes 138, 97, and 207 are short scoots to get to Route 16 but watch the tricky intersection where Route 138 crosses Route 69 and heads down and to the right onto a great little whoop-de-do stretch. You can fly on Route 16 south with soft bends and slow rollers till you reach Colchester. Route 85 merges in and out of town fast, so drive slow and watch for the **Hide-A-Way Café** on the left. Owner Walt Sanchi has been there twenty-five years catering to the locals as well as a stray journalist or two. He recommends his own burgers which are slow-cooked "to retain the juice," giving you plenty of time for a game of pool or darts or a tune on the jukebox. The place is filled with trophies for every kind of team imaginable and the regulars at the bar are more than happy to tell you about them.

Take the immediate right after you go under Route 2. It feels like you're going to grab the cloverleaf onto Route 2, but at the T, bear left onto Lake

One man's castle is another man's folly at Gillette's Castle.

Shore Road. This is a shady, narrow lake-hugging road. The lake is inviting; the signs saying PRIVATE BEACH are not. I stopped at the third little beach, got a couple of stares from the more uptight folk, but no hassles. The water felt great, probably more so for being forbidden fruit.

The **Devil's Hopyard State Park** off of Haywardville Road offers a large park, campground, and a 60-foot waterfall.

The park is considered hallowed ground by the superstitious. The local folklore centers on the Devil's liking of wild and rugged scenery, embracing the park as his (or is that hers?). The other tale is of a traveler who, passing along the trail near a clearing where the hops were growing, saw mist-shrouded forms leaping from the ledges and trees in the hopyard. Zip that tent up tight!

From the superstitious we go to the superfluous: **Gillette's Castle** in East Haddam. From Route 82 west, follow signs to the castle. William Gillette, an actor, is credited with introducing Sherlock Holmes to American theater. He began construction of his castle in 1914 and finished in 1919. Two hundred feet above the Connecticut River, with granite walls four to five feet thick and 24 rooms, Gillette's home reflects his eccentricity. He even built his own three-mile railroad to take guests down to the river. The grounds are extensive and very well cared for, so if you are in a picnic mood, this would be a good place to spend a little time.

Picking up Route 82 west brings you to the Connecticut River and the actual town of East Haddam, which boasts the **Goodspeed Opera House,** a fully restored Victorian theater built in 1876 and offering films, musicals, and plays throughout the spring, summer, and fall. The shows *Man of La Mancha* and *Annie* had their first performances here. If you are interested in theatre, catch one of the backstage tours that are offered. Next door is The **Gelston House** which has a nice patio overlooking the river for outdoor dining as well as a few picnic tables.

The bridge next to the Goodspeed Opera House opens for passing ships by pivoting on its center support. Make sure the road matches up with the bridge before crossing the river, and drive slowly over the steel deck. Then head into the quaint village of Chester.

Route 148 west gets us back to our riding roots. The road is squiggly, has little traffic, and is smooth. Route 79 south points us straight to the sea with several options available for the trip home depending on your time and interests.

Route 1 east/north, the shore road from Madison to Niantic, is a good place to do your errands. This is a commercial strip with plenty of places to buy your supplies at low cost, high-volume stores. **Willoughby's Coffee and Tea** in the town of Madison comes highly recommended for good java and homemade pastry, and you're apt to see a few other two-wheelers lined up in front during good weather. Once your shopping is out of the way, if you've got time for a dip in the ocean, the public beach at **Hammonasset State Park** is especially nice.

Returning to home base, a couple of side roads off of Route 1 break up the commercial flow and bring you closer to the water. Route 154 dips quickly into Fenwick and Saybrook Point, known for good bird watching and its nice boardwalk, before rejoining Route 1 in Old Saybrook. The **Dock and Dine Restaurant** at Saybrook Point is right on the water and a good place to catch a bite to eat and watch the boat traffic on the river. Route 156 does the same type of dip as Route 154 just after the Connecticut River crossing. You can continue on Route 156 into New London, grab Interstate 95 north, drop down to Route 1, and retrace the previous Inland Loop.

Or, if the day is young and you're wanting a different experience, turn left from Route 79 south onto Route 80 east at North Madison for 9.5 miles to

The Dock and Dine Restaurant at Saybrook Point is a great spot to catch a bite to eat (perhaps literally if you're lucky) and watch the sunset over the water.

the Ivoryton/Centerbrook turnoff. Continue straight through both towns onto Route 154 south to the **Essex Steam Train and Riverboat Ride.** This working railroad yard will transport you to a different age, where time doesn't matter too much. Enjoy the half-hour train ride to Deep River Landing where you can board an authentic riverboat for an hour-long cruise. You'll get the river's eye view of what you've already seen on two wheels: Gillette's Castle, Goodspeed Opera House, the Haddam Swing Bridge, and if you're lucky, some of the nesting eagles on the river. Both rides are narrated to point out the nature and history of the area. After the boat trip, hop back on Route 154 south and return to home base on either Route 1 east/north as described above, or on I-95 if you've run out of time and need to hustle home to camp.

Places of Interest

CONNECTICUT

Colchester

Hide-A-Way Café, Route 85, 06415. Phone 860-537-2554. Open Daily 9:00 a.m. to 1:00 a.m. except Sunday 11:00 a.m. to 1:00 a.m. Here's a locals' bar that's friendly and good for a game of darts or pool after your lunch. $

East Haddam

Devil's Hopyard State Park, 366 Hopyard Road, 06423, north of Route 82 off of Haywardville Road. A remote place to camp or rest a weary traveler's bones!

Gillette's Castle, 67 River Rd, 06423, off Route 82. Phone 860-526-2336. www.friendsctstateparks.net/parks/gillette_castle.htm. Open end of May to October, 10.00 a.m. to 4:30 p.m. Expansive views of the Connecticut River from the towers of a medieval castle, this is a great spot for a picnic lunch. Admission $4.

Goodspeed Opera House, Route 82, 06423. Phone 860-873-8668 for tickets; office 860-873-8664. www.goodspeed.org. April through December. Office hours are 9:00 a.m. to 6:30 p.m. Performances as scheduled. Tour a vintage theatre dedicated to preserving the tradition of the American musical theatre.

Essex

Steam Train and Riverboat Ride, 1 Railroad Avenue, 06426. Phone 860-767-0103 or 800-377-3987. www.essexsteamtrain.com. Open daily June to September 10:30 a.m. to 5:30 p.m. and for numerous special events October to May. Ride both the rails and the river through the beautiful Connecticut Valley. Admission $18.50 for train and boat ride.

Groton

USS Nautilus Memorial and Submarine Force Museum, Crystal Lake Road, 06340, off Route 12. Phone 800-343-0079. www.submarinemuseum.com. Open year-round; May 15 to October 31, 9:00 a.m. to 5:00 p.m. Wednesday to Monday and 1:00 p.m. to 5:00 p.m. on Tuesday; 9:00 a.m. to 4:00 p.m. rest of the year. Free. Everything you wanted to know about submarines and their history is here.

Madison

Willoughby's Coffee and Tea, Route 1, 06443, in center of town. Phone 203-245-1600. Open Monday to Saturday 7:00 a.m. to 6:00 p.m and Sunday 8:00 a.m. to 5:00 p.m. If you crave great java and homemade pastries, this is the place.

Mashantucket

Foxwoods Resort and Casino, Route 2, 06339. Phone 800-752-9244. www.foxwoods.com. Open year-round 24/7. See "the wonder of it all" at one of the world's largest gaming casinos.

Mohegan Sun, Route 2E, 06339. Phone 888-226-7711. www.mohegansun.com. Open year-round 24/7. Visit another "world of nonstop thrills and action-packed games" just around the corner from Foxwoods.

Pequot Museum and Research Center, 110 Pequot Trail, 06339. Phone 800-411-9671. www.mashantuket.com. Open daily 9:00 a.m. to 4:00 p.m. Admission $12. Trace the rich cultural heritage and history of Native Americans in New England.

Mystic

Mystic Aquarium, 55 Coogan Boulevard, 06355. Phone 860-572-5955. www.mysticaquarium.org. Open July to Labor Day 9:00 a.m. to 7:00 p.m. daily. Admission $16. From sea creatures to deep sea exploration, there's "always something new, so dive in."

Mystic Seaport, 50 Greenmanville Avenue (Route 27), 06355. Phone 203-527-0711 or 888-9SEAPORT. www.mysticseaport.org. Open year-round, April to October 9:00 a.m. to 5:00 p.m.; November to March 10:00 a.m. to 4:00 p.m. Explore an operational turn-of-the-century seaport and museum. Admission $17.

Pomfret

The Vanilla Bean Café, Corner of Routes 169, 44, and 97, 06258. Phone 860-928-1562. www.thevanillabeancafe.com. This popular local café owned by a motorcycling family was voted "Top Stop" four years in a row by the local Harley riders. $$

Saybrook Point

Dock and Dine Restaurant, Saybrook Point, 06475. Phone 860-388-4665. Open 11:30 a.m. to 9:00 p.m. year-round except closed Monday and Tuesday in winter. Known for its seafood and great view of the river, this spot is the place to be at sunset.

Stonington

Old Light House Museum, 7 Water Street, 06378. Phone 860-535-1440. Open May 1 to October 31, 10:00 a.m. to 5:00 p.m. Climb to the top of the lighthouse for a 360-degree view of Long Island Sound. Admission $2.

Woodstock Valley

Stoggy Hollow Restaurant and General Store, Route 198, 06282. Phone 860-974-3814. Sit on the open deck, enjoy a perfect deli sandwich, and watch the two-wheel action on the road below. $$

MASSACHUSETTS

Fall River

Battleship Cove and Fall River Heritage State Park, Davol Street, 02721. Phone 800-533-3194 and 508-675-5759 respectively. www.battleshipcove.com. Open year-round except major holidays. Times vary with seasons. Enjoy the world's largest collection of historic naval ships. Admission $10. AAA discount.

Marine Museum at Fall River, 70 Water Street, 02721. Phone 508-674-3533. www.marinemuseum.org. Open year-round, Monday to Friday 9:00 a.m. to 5:00 p.m., Saturday noon to 5:00 p.m., Sunday noon to 4:00 p.m. If you're a *Titanic* or old steamship buff, this is your place. Admission $5.

Waterstreet Café, 36 Water Street, 02721. Phone 508-672-8748. www.waterstreetcafe.com. Serving lunch and dinner every day and brunch on Sunday from 10:30 a.m. to 3:00 p.m. $$

New Bedford

New Bedford Whaling Museum, 18 Johnny Cake Hill, 02740. Phone 508-997-0046. www.whalingmuseum.org. Open daily year-round 9:00 a.m. to 5:00 p.m. except major holidays. Admission $8. AAA discount. See the world's largest ship model, a 66-foot skeleton of a rare blue whale, and many other fascinating exhibits from the great age of whaling.

Seamen's Bethel, Johnny Cake Hill, 02740, across from the Whaling Museum. Phone 508-992-3295. Open May to October 10:00 a.m. to 5:00 p.m., November to April, Monday to Friday 11:00 a.m. to 1:00 p.m. and until 5:00 p.m. on the weekends. If you are here, then be there to learn a little bit of literary history. Be sure to read all the plaques of seamen lost! Donations accepted.

Westport

Horseneck Beach State Reservation, Westport Point, 02791. Phone 508-636-8816. Open mid-May to mid-October. This is a popular spot for both camping and beaching. Admission is $5 for the beach and $12 for a campsite.

RHODE ISLAND

Charlestown

Burlingame State Park, U.S. Route 1, 02813. Phone 401-332-8910 or 401-332-7337 for campsite info. www.riparks.com. Excellent, spacious campground with 733 sites, open from April 15 to October 31. Fee $10.

Jamestown

Beavertail Lighthouse and State Park, Beavertail Road, 02835. Phone 401-423-3270. www.beavertaillight.org. Lighthouse is open June to August; Park open year-round. Beautiful views and good spots to rest by the ocean's edge await you and the steed. Donations accepted.

Jamestown Harbor

East Ferry Market & Deli, 47 Cononicus Avenue, 02835. Phone 401-423-1592. Daily 6:30 a.m. to 5:00 p.m. Great coffee, pastries, and a perfect location for reading the morning paper and watching the boats in the harbor are here. $$

Misquamicut

Misquamicut State Beach, Atlantic Avenue. www.riparks.com. Open late June to Labor Day 9:00 a.m. to 6:00 p.m. This is an unattended open stretch of beach, where Beach Blanket Bingo Bonanza meets Honky-Tonk City. Fee $12.

Newport

Castle Hill Inn, 590 Ocean Dr., 02840. Phone 401-849-3800 or 888-466-1355. www.castlehill.com. The views are unsurpassed from the backyard and patio. $$$

The Mansions, Bellevue Avenue, 02840. www.newportmansions.org. Information for any or all of the mansions can be obtained by calling 401-847-1000. Open May to September daily. Varies by mansion at other times. Do one at least! Admission is

Sitting on the patio of the Inn at Castle Hill, you can watch great ships entering and leaving Newport Harbor.

pricey and varies by mansion and how many you are visiting, but it's well worth the expense.

Newport Harbor Hotel and Marina, 49 America's Cup Ave, 02840. Phone 401-847-9000 or 800-955-2558. www.nhhm.com. Splurge on a room with a harbor view. $$$

Newport Transportation and Visitor's Information Center, 23 America's Cup Ave, 02840. Phone 401-845-9123 or 800-976-5122. www.GoNewport.com. These folks can get you a room with a view to suit your budget and recommend tours, restaurants, and other things to see and do.

Red Parrot Restaurant, 348 Thames Street 02840. Phone 401-847-3800 or 401-847-3140. www.redparrotrestaurant.com. Open Daily. Good food, decadent desserts, and the best location in town await at this popular Newport restaurant.

Index

Other Titles in the Whitehorse Press
Motorcycle Journeys Series
(visit us at www.whitehorsepress.com)

Motorcycle Journeys Through California

by Clement Salvadori
Sftbd., 5-1/2 x 8-1/2 in., 320 pp., color
Order code: MJCA (ISBN 1-884313-18-3)
Price: $24.95
This book is about roads—sweeping roads high along the coast, lonely roads amidst desert splendor, and sporting twisties through grand forests—superb routes that offer some of the best year-round riding in the world.

Motorcycle Journeys Through the Alps & Corsica, Third Edition

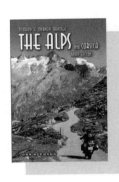

by John Hermann
Sftbd., 5-1/2 x 8-1/2 in., 352 pp., color
Order code: HERM3 (ISBN 1-884313-32-9)
Price: $24.95
This third edition is the *creme de la creme* of Alpine touring—now in full color. Maps, images, graphics, and witty and insightful text leave you no excuse at all not to buy this and go!

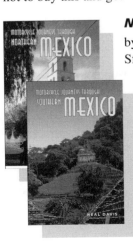

Motorcycle Journeys Through Mexico

by Neal Davis
Sftbd., 5-1/2 x 8-1/2 in., b/w
Order code: MJNM (ISBN 1-884313-20-5)
and MJSM (ISBN 1-884313-26-4)
Price: $19.95 each
Join Neal Davis as he leads two-wheeled tours through the varied wonders of Mexico. The rich history and culture of Mexico have given our southern neighbor a unique flavor that is best appreciated first-hand—and motorcycling makes that possible like no other method of travel.

Order toll-free at 800-531-1133

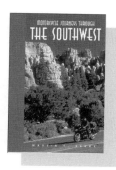

Motorcycle Journeys Through the Southwest

by Marty Berke
Sftbd., 5-1/2 x 8-1/2 in., 430 pp., b/w
Order code: MJSW (ISBN 0-9621834-9-0)
Price: $19.95
Marty Berke is back with his guide to the American Southwest, where mountains, desert, roads, and sunny weather combine for ideal riding.

Motorcycle Journeys Through the Appalachians

by Dale Coyner
Sftbd., 5-1/2 x 8-1/2 in., 320 pp., b/w
Order code: COYN (ISBN 1-884313-02-7)
Price: $19.95
Dale Coyner leads you in exploring the scenic mountain vistas and bucolic valleys of a part of the country that's historically rich, culturally diverse, and laced with enticing roads.

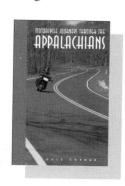

Motorcycle Journeys Through Baja

by Clement Salvadori
Sftbd., 5-1/2 x 8-1/2 in., 240 pp., b/w
Order code: SALV (ISBN 1-884313-08-6)
Price: $19.95
Join Clement Salvadori as he personally leads you on an entertaining tour South of the Border. From TJ to Cabo, Salvadori knows Baja, having explored this grand peninsula regularly for more than 20 years.

Motorcycle Vagabonding in Japan

by Guy de la Rupelle
Sftbd., 5-1/2 x 8-1/2 in., 256 pp., b/w
Order code: MVJ (ISBN 1-884313-16-7)
Price: $19.95
Resident author Guy de La Rupelle has found terrific roads to wander in the "Land of the Rising Sun." Sample the culture that Japan has to offer without the hassle of crowds, traffic, stress, and consumerism.

About the Author

Marty Berke wrote *Motorcycle Journeys Through New England* out of a life-long love of the open road. A resident of Mexico Beach, Florida, he caught the two-wheeled touring bug with his first Schwinn, and graduated to the motorized species not long afterward with a 1955 Vespa, a driver's license, and a $50 IOU to Mom.

After graduating from C.W. Post College with a degree in economics, Marty joined the international division of a large high-tech corporation and spent fifteen years pursuing his hobby—touring—while setting up new businesses and marketing programs throughout Europe, the Americas, the South Pacific, and Asia.

Marty, an MSF instructor, now focuses on finding good roads all over the world and new ways to share them with you. Check out his book *Motorcycle Journeys Through the Southwest,* if your plans take you to that palace of riding pleasure.